NOT UNTO DEATH
MY STORY

Written by Ruth Santiago

TRILOGY
PROFESSIONAL PUBLISHING MEETS POWERFUL PROMOTION

A wholly owned subsidiary of **TBN**

Not Unto Death
My Story
Trilogy Christian Publishers
A Wholly Owned Subsidary of Trinity Broadcasting Network
2442 Michelle Drive
Tustin, CA 92780
Copyright © 2022 by **Ruth Santiago**

Scripture quotations marked (KJV) taken from *The Holy Bible, King James Version.* Cambridge Edition: 1769.

For information, address Trilogy Christian Publishing Rights Department, 2442 Michelle Drive, Tustin, CA 92780.

10 9 8 7 6 5 4 3 2 1

Library of Congress Cataloging-in-Publication Data is available.
ISBN: 978-1-68556-859-7
ISBN: 978-1-68556-860-3

DEDICATIONS

This book is, firstly, dedicated to my Lord and Savior Jesus Christ who walked my family and I through a journey which we never dreamed we'd have to go through. He (Jesus) took our hand in His, never letting go until He brought us out safely to the other side. He was and has remained faithful. He has been glorified and continues to do so.

Secondly, to my husband, Joe Santiago, who has been one of the godliest men I know. He was a rock and a constant source of strength for me as we took this journey together.

Lastly, to my children Enid, Jaysen, and Jeanette; they too journeyed with us. Though their faith was sorely tested they were and remain faithful not only to us, their parents, but to their Lord and Savior Jesus Christ.

PREFACE

This book has been inspired by a journey our family was forced to travel. The Lord clearly spoke to me these words "Write your story." It wasn't easy to relive this journey we as a family had to travel, however the Lord impressed on my heart time and time and again over the years that it was needed. People needed to hear that the God that I served was a good God. They needed to hear that He (God) is faithful and will remain faithful no matter what they may be going through. The Lord used me as a vessel to convey this message to all who pick up a copy of this book. They will not go away disappointed instead they will get a glimpse of the magnitude of His love for all His creation.

ACKNOWLEDGEMENT

This book would never have gone to print had it not been for a benefactor who wants to remain anonymous, believing in "not letting the left hand know what the right hand is doing." They believed in the book and its story; believing that is has the power to encourage and possibly help bring comfort to someone who's journey is just beginning or has finished their journey having been left with many unanswered questions. This benefactor generously gave the necessary funds to have the book published. What you give in secret, God will reward you openly and has been acknowledged in heaven, but I want to say thank you publicly!

INTRODUCTION

The question most people will be asking is: why did you wait so long to write this book, Not Unto Death, My Story? Good question. I, myself, pondered this question many times. I would begin to write, and I'd hit a brick wall. Some would call that writer's block. I say it was the Lord; the Lord's timing is perfect. He knew when this story, this book, would be most effective. When it would minister to those who would read it. Thus, time needed to pass so that the words that were spoken to me so many years ago would be fulfilled and, therefore, I could say with full assurance: John 11:4 "this sickness is not unto death but for the glory of God, that the Son of God might be glorified thereby..." (KJV) Truly, the Lord has been and continues to be glorified; it will be evident to you as you read the book.

CHAPTER 1

We all have dreams of living that enchanted life. At least I did! When you meet your prince charming, he sweeps you off your feet and you ride into the sunset together, a life of total bliss and happiness. I know that was my dream. I really thought I had found my prince charming. But after eleven years of marriage, the ivory tower I had constructed in my mind, came tumbling down, along with the marriage. My prince charming, Jose Santiago, after eleven years of marriage and three children, informed me that he was no longer in love with me. You see, it was my castle, my ivory tower, but not his. I was a control freak and a perfectionist and Joe had had enough. He wanted out. I was so broken, so shattered. That brokenness led me to the foot of Calvary; it's a place where lost and broken people arrive when they come to the end of self. That's where I found myself, completely without hope.

My world revolved around my job, my home, my children, my husband, and what people thought of me. I was living a very shallow life, though I didn't know it at the time. Having no one to really turn to, I turned to the

God that I had been introduced to as a child. I remember sitting on the front steps of our home at 89 Arnold Street Staten Island, N.Y. I cried out to the Lord in desperation. I asked Him to take the broken pieces of my life and do whatever He wanted to do with them. I also asked the Lord to kill my husband; yes, I was serious about that. You see in my selfishness, I felt that I had helped Joe climb the corporate ladder and I was not about to let some other woman reap the benefits of my hard work. Looking back, I realized how full of myself I had become. But in spite of that, God proved to be faithful; He answered my prayer and killed my husband, though not it in the physical sense of the word, as you will later see.

At that time my sister-in-law, Aida, had been on a spiritual journey. She had heard of a new church in Staten Island called Calvary Tabernacle (later changed to The International Christian Center) and asked me if I would go with her. Little did we know that this was going to be a divine appointment for me. The Lord used her hunger for the truth to bring me to Himself. I will forever be grateful to her because she was instrumental in my coming to Christ.

I went with Aida to visit the church. They were in the process of building a sanctuary and were renting an empty drug store in Highland Blvd, Staten Island while the building was being completed. I asked my husband to drive me since at the time I didn't drive. Reluctantly, he drove Aida, my mom, and I to church. Before we attended the service, I discovered that this was a Pentecostal church. As I child, I had been raised in the Pentecostal church and remembered how legalistic they were (that was my experience). So, I removed all my makeup and put on huge sunglasses to cover my unmade face. After all I wasn't about to be seen without makeup. That evening, we entered this makeshift church. Folding chairs were used for seating, which had to be set up and taken down after each service. I will never forget entering that place. I saw people so enthralled in the presence of the Lord. Their hands and gaze were lifted towards Heaven. Tears flowed from many faces, as they were enveloped in the presence of what could only be described as love; a love that was tangible.

In spite of the unsophisticated surroundings, I felt a presence that I had never felt before. I had a difficult time staying composed. Tears began to flow from my eyes and down my cheeks. Tears that now were uncontrollable. Suddenly, this all put together woman who lived for total control, was totally undone, and I mean undone. I wanted to run out, especially when someone began to speak in tongues. I had come full circle and was face to face with the God I had been running from all my life.

The Pastor was away that evening. As fill in, they had a video testimony of B.J. Thomas, a famous singer at the time. To this day I can't remember a word he said, I was so undone by worship. I do remember that they had an altar call; I clung with clinched fingers to my chair. However, to my surprise, as if I had been transported to the front, there I was front and center, wailing; not crying, not weeping, but wailing beyond control. That night thirty-seven years ago, I surrendered everything to the Lord and committed my life totally to Him. Again, I repeated the same words I had spoken to the Lord in front of my house weeks earlier, "Lord take the broken pieces of my life and do whatever you want with them; and kill my husband." Aren't you glad that God has a sense of humor? Naturally, He didn't kill him physically. However, He answered my prayer by gloriously saving him six months later. Having seen such a wonderful transformation in my life, he gave his life totally to the Lord. Scripture says in Romans 2:4, God's kindness is intended to lead us to repentance. I loved the Lord with all my heart, and I showed Joe that unconditional love. The Lord saved us both, healed our marriage and filled us both with His holy Spirit. So began our journey with Christ. With our marriage totally restored; our children, Enid - eleven, Jaysen - seven and our youngest, Jeanette, not quite two at the time, we now had a Christ centered home. Our two oldest, Enid and Jaysen, saw the radical change in our lives and they, too, embraced Christ as their Savior. Life was wonderful. This was not a fairy tale; it was a home that embodied Christ in all that we did. We were truly whole, enjoying the Lord's peace and presence every day.

At that time, the Lord began to prompt Joe and I to move to Swedesboro, a small town in southern New Jersey. It was so small, if you blinked, you'd miss it. The downtown area was really quaint. There were no streetlights and there were farms as far as the eye could see. Ironically, my brother and sister-in-law in law (another one of Joe's sisters) lived there. Every time we visited; I would comment: "I never want to live in such a small town." I'd lived in New York all my life; a New Yorker through and through, at least I was at the time I said that.

The Lord continued to prompt us to move. We wanted to make sure what we heard was from the Lord. We had read in the Bible the story of Gideon when the Lord asked him to lead the children of Israel against their enemy the Midianites. Gideon asked the Lord to confirm His word. So, he took a fleece and asked the Lord to cause the fleece to be saturated, but the ground around it to be dry. Then he asked to Lord to cause the ground to be saturated but the fleece dry. The Lord did as Gideon requested. As innocent new Christians, we figured, if it worked for Gideon, surely it would work for us. In Christian circles this is called "putting out a fleece" So we prayed and asked the Lord, that if He was truly leading us to move to Swedesboro, that He would do the following things; first, that He would find a buyer for our home; second, that the buyer would be Christian; and third, that we would get a buyer within a week (that's right within a week). The reason we asked for a Christian buyer was that Joe's family and my mother were living on the same street; it was so important to us to leave a light, a Christian witness that would be a blessing to our parents, as well as to the community.

We chose not to get a realtor or advertise, again, so as to prove that our venture was in line with the leading of the Holy Spirit. We depended totally on the Lord to orchestrate not only the selling of our old home, but the purchase of our new home. If within that week no one came forth to buy our home and the buyer would be a Christian, we would consider the prompting not to be from the Lord and we would stay in Staten Island.

We prayed on a Tuesday. Thursday of that same week Joe called me from work. He informed me that one of his co-workers had gotten saved recently. Joe was anxious to speak with him since he and his coworker had been long time adversaries. During their conversation, his coworker, named Johnny Williams, mentioned that he had been praying for the Lord to find him place to live; primarily, he was looking for a home. When Joe mentioned that we were selling our home, Johnny asked if he could come by and see it. As Joe spoke to me, I felt my spirit leap with excitement. Johnny Williams came to see our home that Saturday and the rest, my friend, is what they call history. He loved the house and committed to buying it on the spot. The Lord answered our prayer, not in seven days, but in three days. Having matured greatly since then in the Lord I don't recommend "putting out a fleece"; you might get fleeced.

Now that our home was under contract, we now needed to find a home. Needless to say, that the Lord was faithful again. We sold our old home and bought and moved into our new home in Swedesboro New Jersey in twenty-eight days; yes, my friend in twenty-eight days. Even our realtor, Jim Baber, said he had never seen a sale go so fast and so smoothly. We knew it was God and we were ready for our next great adventure, as were our children.

CHAPTER 2

The transition for our children went smoothly. We found a great church not five minutes from our home, Beckett Community Church. We quickly became involved. Though I was a relatively new Christian, the Lord had His hand on my life, and I was asked to teach Sunday School. I jumped at the opportunity to be used by the Lord. This time was both a challenging and rewarding time. I truly believed we were living a wonderfully blessed life.

As time went on, I would transition from teaching Sunday School to leading the Women's Ministry in our church. As He had done before, the Lord blessed the work He gave me to do. Our children were attending a Christian School and they were also growing in their faith and relationship with the Lord.

As time passed, I became so burdened with the youth of our church. At the time there was no youth pastor. I prayed for them continually. For over two years I asked the Lord to send someone who would step up to the plate and minister to them. I don't know if you know this, but

I know it all too well, the Lord has a sense of humor. On this particular day, I had driven my husband Joe to work. He was now working in Wilmington, Delaware. After many years of commuting to New York, he finally got a job twenty minutes from home. We were a one car family, and I needed the car to run errands, so I dropped Joe off at work and headed home. As I was crossing the Delaware Memorial Bridge, I was listening to a Christian radio station. They were announcing a youth rally. Once again, my mind and my heart were drawn to the youth of our church. I prayed, "Lord, send someone to minister to our young people." I even had the audacity to say to the Lord; "Lord, if you want, I'll take them to this event." No sooner had I said that, that I heard the voice of the Lord say, "I want you to lead the youth." I almost crashed my car; I was so shocked. But the prompting was so strong that I had a dialogue with Lord that went something like this: "Lord I will go home, call, Pastor Petrucci and see if he will see me. If he can't, at least I tried."

As soon as I agreed to speak with the pastor, it was as if I had had a teleprompter in front of me; the Lord showed be exactly what I was to say when I met with the pastor. The Lord even showed me what I would be doing with the youth. He gave me His vision for the youth of the church. I was amazed and scared to death at the same time. I was comfortable ministering to women, but not to youth. They are so complicated. Did I really have what it takes? I wasn't sure.

I got home and called the pastor before I lost my

nerve. And wouldn't you know it? He had a free slot and would love for me to come over and chat. So, on my way, I went. I sat down and began to share my burden for our youth. Pastor told me that he had a couple he was considering as potential youth pastor candidates. I felt I had dodged a bullet. However, the Lord prompted me to ask for permission to share my heart and what the Lord had shown me. As I shared what the Lord had laid on my heart, pastor's eyes became teary, and I knew I was in trouble. After having heard me out, he proceeded to tell me that I could take over the youth program. And so began one of the greatest, most fulfilling, exciting, and at the same time, the scariest adventure of my life.

In spite of the fact I felt so ill prepared, the Holy Spirit equipped me and blessed the ministry. The very first thing the Lord instructed me to do was to take the youth on a mission's trip. I joined up with a church in San Diego called Sun City and off we went on our very first mission's trip to Tijuana, Mexico. Our team was quite small compared to the other teams. Our team consisted of my son Jaysen. my nephew Lenny; two brothers, Tommy and Stephen Franks; and Don Roach.

Knowing my limitations, (never having undertaken such a task) and led by the Holy Spirit, we used our time to fast and pray. We also took time to prepare the materials needed to minister to the kids in Tijuana. Most of the ministry involved doing VBS (Vacation Bible Studies). God proved Himself totally faithful and we were able to raise all the funds needed for the trip. The young men saw, firsthand, God's provision as we lacked nothing for the trip. This whole experience helped to strengthen their faith and we were assured that this trip was totally ordained of God. The trip was a complete success as we saw many come to know the Lord, was well as fed many of the poor that village.

As a novice, I depended totally on the Lord and His leading. Having the blessing and support of my husband, the youth were finally growing spiritually. They became a very tightly knit group. They loved and respected each other. They were being used by the Lord to minister in our church, and were invited to minister in other churches as well; even to churches from different denominations. It was an exciting time, filled with great promise. I was so fulfilled, so blessed; life couldn't get any better.

CHAPTER 3

While I ministered to the youth of our church, my oldest child, Enid, began to struggle in her faith. Her relationship with the Lord began to get cold. She was torn between the Lord, and the world and her friends. Enid was a beautiful young woman with an amazing personality and sense of humor. Everyone who met her instantly liked her. At the time, she was attending high school at The Christian Academy in Media, PA. She had been hanging out with several friends who, though attending the same school, didn't really have a real personal relationship with the Lord. Satan is everywhere. He even visits churches every Sunday and, as we soon found out, he also visits schools. These friends weren't bad. They just didn't believe the way we did, and they began to influence our daughter's spiritual life. She would spend one evening a week with this friend in Media PA., supposedly, to attend a Bible study. However, she was actually coming back into New Jersey to attend a night club which on Tuesdays closed their bars and catered to youth. They could hang out and dance. Though not allowed to consume alcoholic beverages, they were being introduced to nightclubbing. Unbeknownst to me, while I was ministering to the youth of our church, the devil was busy enticing my daughter to the nightlife. She continued to attend Saturday night youth services, participated in all our activities, and attended Sunday services so we assumed she was okay.

It was at this club she met a young man who swept her off her feet. She introduced him to us as a young Christian man she had met at her Bible study class on Tuesdays. Again, trusting that she was being honest, we welcomed this young man into our home. However, after almost two years of what had been very turbulent relationship (as we found out later), she ended her relationship with him, and life became somewhat normal.

Enid always wanted to so become a cosmetologist, so after she graduated high school, she applied and was accepted into Gloucester County Institute of Technology's (GCIT) cosmetology program. In order to pay for her tuition, she applied for a job at our local vet's office and was hired. This, by the way, was a perfect fit for her as she loved animals, with the exceptions of reptiles. She registered and paid her own tuition to cosmetology school.

Enid's life seemed to be heading in the right direction. However, I still sensed she was struggling in her relationship with the Lord. So as any good parent would do, both Joe and I prayed continually for her.

I continued to minister to our youth. As was my custom, I would get up every day around 5:00 in the morning and head to our church to pray for the ministry the Lord had entrusted into my hands. One particular morning, I was at the altar praying. As I prayed, I had what I could only describe as a vision. As I prayed in the Spirit, I saw a knight enter the sanctuary. He was dressed in black, had a black javelin in his hand and was mounted on an ebony black stallion. The horse raised his front legs and began to trot towards me. As I prayed the Holy Spirit instructed me not look back; just continue to pray and rebuke the enemy. I did as I was directed. The horse stopped dead in its tracks and again not turning but seeing in the Spirit, the knight backed out of the sanctuary slowly as I prayed. As he began to exit, he suddenly stopped and made his way through the two rows of chairs which were to my left; the chairs normally occupied by the youth.

The knight eventually left the sanctuary and the vision ended. I knelt there and thanked the Lord for His divine protection, not fully understanding what the vision meant. I felt that rebuking the knight was all that I needed to do. So, I finished praying and went home. I did share the vision with my husband, and we felt that the victory had been won and didn't think about it again.

Our daughter Enid continued to struggle with her faith. She wasn't doing anything overtly bad, but I just sensed she was going through the motions. She wasn't choosing her friends wisely and that concerned Joe and I, so we continued to pray for her. Enid was not involved in drugs; she had never smoked; to our knowledge she had never drank nor been sexually promiscuous. She was a good decent young woman. The problem was and still is, being good will not get you to heaven. Only a personal relationship with Christ and a life pleasing to Him can gain you access into His kingdom.

Our desire for all our children, from the moment we became Christians, was that they encounter Christ in a very personal way. We did the very best we knew to do: we had devotions daily; we enrolled them in Christian School; and had a good church which we attended together regularly. We did our due diligence to ensure they were exposed to the Word of God daily. However, as a young adult, Enid had to make her own a decision to follow Christ. She attended services with us regularly. However, she was neglecting her personal devotional life. That is all Satan needs to introduce you to worldly friends and activities. Before you know it, he has his claws in you and you don't even know it. This was the case with our daughter. The Word of God calls this, having a form of godliness, but denying the power thereof (2 Timothy 3:5). A lukewarm Christian is the devil's playground. The book of Revelation (3:16) tells us that if we are lukewarm, He (God) will spew us out of His mouth. Our daughter was in danger of being spewed out of the Lord's mouth.

As a youth pastor, there is no greater struggle than seeing other young people embracing the Lord's presence and seeing your child straying farther and farther away from the Him. I knew I had been called to minister to the youth of our church. God had clearly anointed me, and I was seeing mighty moves of God within our youth group. Young people being baptized in the Holy Spirit and their lives radically changed. Still, I ached seeing my oldest daughter in the fringes. I prayed constantly for her. I knew that the enemy was licking at her heels and she, unknowingly, was opening herself to his advances by the friends she was keeping and the places she was going.

CHAPTER 4

It's like the enemy to attack when you are most vulnerable. So just at the right moment, when our daughter wasn't walking with the Lord, only going through the motions, he attacked. Enid had been losing weight for some time but refused to see a doctor. At twenty-one years of age, it was impossible to force her to do that. So, I did what any good mother would do, I committed her to the Lord, and I prayed daily for her. For several years she had struggled with a skin rash and had gone to see a dermatologist who told her she had eczema. The doctor prescribed an ointment which seemed to alleviate the symptoms for a while. The rash, however, came back and never really healed. For a season it would go away and then it would flare up again. She just learned to live with the skin rash because it wasn't severe.

As time went on, she began to have difficulty sleeping. She would wake up in the morning with very swollen eyes. She again refused to go see a doctor. It was now several weeks since she began experiencing these symptoms and I finally convinced her to go see her primary physician,

Dr S. He examined her, but he didn't feel it was anything to be alarmed about and sent her home. So, we were back to square one. It was evident that there was something terribly wrong, but what? Days had come and gone since Enid had gone to the doctor. Enid hadn't gotten any worse, so she assumed she was okay; probably just bad allergies.

I noticed that Enid continued to lose weight. She was thin to begin with, but she just seemed thinner than usual. I addressed the issue with her again. She assured me that she was eating and that she was fine. Enid was twenty-one years old. I knew that she wasn't going to allow to be hogtied and force fed, so I had to accept what she had told me at face value.

So often, days come and go, and we give little thought about what a day can bring. Such was the case on Tuesday, March 29th 1994. I was scheduled to go out to lunch with my friend Phyllis. Jaysen and Jeanette, our other two children, were in school and Enid was at work at the local vet's office in Swedesboro, New Jersey. My friend Phyllis had arrived, and we were just about to leave, when the phone rang. It was Enid; she said that she was having difficulty breathing. She explained that every time she bent down, she felt like her breathing pathway, her trachea was being covered by something which made it difficult for her to breathe. As we were having this conversation, I heard the audible voice of the enemy say, "I'm going to kill your daughter." I rebuked him immediately and continued my conversation with my daughter.

As quickly as I heard those words from the enemy, the

Lord spoke to my heart: John 11:4, "this sickness is not unto death but for the glory of God, that the Son of God might be glorified thereby..." (KJV). I told my daughter to hang up, that I would call the doctor and get back to her. My head was reeling, my mind went back to several weeks before when she had gone to her primary physician with similar symptoms and he had dismissed them, suggesting it was her imagination. Enid had always been the picture of health. She didn't drink, didn't smoke, had never done drugs, so she figured she would be fine and let it go. As I had said before, she wasn't a big fan of doctors, especially when her doctor inferred that it was all in her mind. Now here she was calling me somewhat concerned. I canceled my lunch date with my friend Phyllis. I decided to pick my daughter up at the Vet and take her straight to the hospital. My friend Phyllis dropped me off since Enid was using my car during the week to get to work. We got in the car, and I rushed her to the emergency room at Underwood Memorial Hospital in Woodbury, New Jersey.

What had started out as a routine Tuesday, suddenly became a nightmare. However, we were awake and living every moment. Enid was taken into one of the cubicles in the emergency room. The first thing they wanted to do was draw blood. Try as they might, they couldn't get a vein. It was as if her veins had retreated, and none could be found. Needless to say, by this time Enid was beyond hysterical. The doctor on call had to give her a mild tranquilizer which helped calm her down. They had to call in a pediatric phlebotomist who was able to draw the blood, the samples needed using a pediatric needle. By this time Enid was somewhat calm. She was then taken to get what is called a soft tissue X-Ray, otherwise called a Neck X-Ray. This procedure uses small amounts of radiation to make images of soft tissues in the neck and hollow parts such as airways, allow X-Ray beams to pass through them and appear black showing any abnormalities.

So, off Enid went to X-Ray and I stood there numb. "What is happening Lord? You have been so faithful." As I waited, I recalled how He had healed our marriage. He relocated us to New Jersey a year later; placed us in a wonderful church; opened doors for ministry to me. "I've been faithful Lord; so, what went wrong? Why am I now in the emergency room of Underwood hospital waiting for the results of blood work and a soft tissue X-Ray for my daughter?" As I pondered these thoughts in my heart, along comes my daughter Enid. The tranquilizer they had given her had taken effect. It had not only calmed her down, but she was also downright giddy. I can still see her as she was being wheeled back into her cubicles laughing and screaming: "Whee Whee!"

We waited for what seemed like an eternity for the doctors to come and give us the results of her labs and X-Rays. Finally, the doctor came into our cubicle and proceeded to tell us that Enid had a mass in her throat that was constricting her air passages; in fact, she was being deprived of oxygen. That is why her nail beds were turning blue; that is a sure sign of oxygen deprivation. Then a surgeon came in and informed me that they needed to do a biopsy to be able to identify the mass.

This time Enid was wheeled into an area that appeared to be a surgical area. I was allowed to stay with her during the procedure. My mind was such a blur I couldn't discern whether this whole scene was real or not. Just before the procedure was about to be done, my sister-in-law Olga arrived. Olga stayed by my side; and how I needed someone right then and there. She was a God send. I have to give her a lot of credit. She is quite squeamish when it comes to blood, but she stood right there by my side as they numbed Enid's chest and aspirated a tissue sample from her chest.

As my beautiful daughter cried, I wanted to go into hysterics, but I couldn't. I just kept remembering John 11:4, "this sickness is not unto death but for the glory of God, that the Son of God might be glorified thereby..." (KJV). I invited the Holy Spirit to comfort Enid and myself while we waited for the results.

I called my husband Joe, who worked in Chester, PA. Joe raced to the hospital and together we sat in the waiting room waiting for the surgeon to come and tell us what was going on. We knew that, even before they spoke to us, they would speak to Enid. She was twenty-one years old and an adult, so they would be speaking to her first. She was alone in a room recovering from the procedure. My heart went out to her; she was twenty-one, but she was still my little girl. I just wanted to take her in my arms and reassure her that everything was going to be okay. I prayed silently that she would be able to handle whatever they had told her or were telling her.

It seemed like forever when Dr. L. stepped into the waiting room. Still in his scrubs, he stood in front of Joe and I and very calmly, without any emotion to speak of, told us that our beautiful daughter Enid, barely an adult, had Non-Hodgkins Lymphoma. He told us that an oncologist was with our daughter explaining the situation; as quickly as he had entered the room, he left. Leaving us completely numb. Non-Hodgkins Lymphoma... what exactly is that? Our beautiful twenty-one-year-old, who had her whole life ahead of her, had a disease we had never even heard of before Enid was about to graduate from cosmetology school, excited about her career. What did this mean to all her plans all her dreams? As I thought silently about our daughter's future, we were escorted to her room. She was sitting up in her bed when we walked in. The surgeon, as well as the oncologist, had already spoken to her. The oncologist was now waiting in the room with our daughter.

When we walked in, Enid extended her arms towards the apple of her eye, her dad. Joe walked over to her and held her in his arms. She buried her head in his chest and wept uncontrollably. I stood there paralyzed by grief, fear, and disbelief. A gamut of emotions, that I couldn't put into words, assaulted my mind. I remember the oncologist, who will go simply as Doctor B, a gentle man in his mid-forties, tried to explain to us what the diagnosis meant and what the course of treatment would be, with absolutely no positive prognosis. As he spoke, I recalled the Word the

Lord had given me, found in John 11:4 "this sickness is not unto death but for the glory of God, that the Son of God might be glorified thereby..." (KJV) I stood on that word.

As the doctor spoke to her, Enid, with her never changing sense of humor told him, "Go away, you make her sweat," was able to diffuse a difficult situation. For a brief moment we all forgot why we were there and laughed; for that moment we were okay.

Our daughter was admitted that night to Underwood Memorial Hospital in very critical condition. Her breathing was labored and had to be put on oxygen. There were no immediate plans to give her treatment; they just wanted to keep her comfortable. We let our church family know what was going on and they began to pray. That evening my brother Nelson and several members of our church came and anointed Enid with oil and prayed the prayer of faith over her. Praise the Lord, she made it through the night. I truly believe that those prayers kept her alive. She truly was at death's door that evening. I believe the doctors didn't think she would make it through the night. We were, however, standing on God's Word John 11:4 "this sickness is not unto death but for the glory of God, that the Son of God might be glorified thereby..." (KJV), and believing for a miracle, which is what we needed.

The following day was Wednesday, and having made it through the night, the oncologist decided to administer the first treatment of chemotherapy. The doctors decided to keep her till Monday to monitor any reactions she may have to the chemo.

Easter was only four days away and our daughter didn't want to be left alone. So, I spent the next couple of days in the hospital with her. I made quick runs home to check on our two children, Jaysen and Jeanette, shower, and change. Thank God for family who watched over Jeanette and Jaysen, allowing Joe and I to spend most of the time in the Hospital with Enid. Our lives had been turned upside down, but we were trying to make the best of it.

Before our daughter left the hospital Monday morning, one of the oncologists on staff, Doctor G., came in and drew a diagram showing us exactly what we were dealing with and told us the severity of her situation; see diagram below.

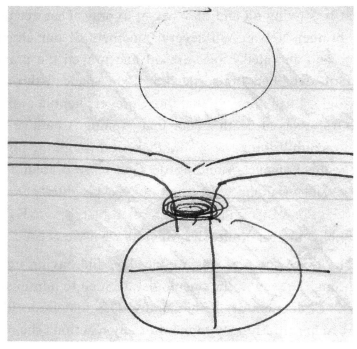

She had a mass wrapped around her air passage, pressing against her heart and lungs. He also explained again what the course of treatments would be. Although he was aware that another oncologist had spoken with us when Enid was admitted, considering how chaotic things were then, he felt it wise to review what had been discussed in the event that we had missed some vital information. He was right! I couldn't grasp what was happening, let alone remember all that had been said our first night there. So, we were very grateful that Dr. G took the time out to re-explain Enid's diagnosis as well as the course of treatment. Again, having heard his dire prognosis I clung onto John 11:4 "this sickness is not unto death but for the glory of God, that the Son of God might be glorified thereby..." (KJV)

We knew nothing about cancer, having never had anyone in our immediate family diagnosed with cancer of any kind. We didn't even know that cancer was diagnosed in stages. The only stages I had ever heard of were the stages actors appeared on. The doctor explained that there were four stages for cancer; our daughter's cancer was in stage three. At this stage the cancer was very aggressive and very difficult to treat. The treatments that they were going to administer was called CHOP; a combination of four drugs: cyclophosphamide, doxorubicin, vincristine, and prednisone. She was to get six treatments. The first was administered in the hospital the previous Wednesday. Then after being released, she would receive the additional treatments every three weeks as an outpatient; her body would need time to recover after each treatment.

It was comforting for my daughter to know that she would only receive her first treatment as an inpatient and the other five as an outpatient. What she wanted more than anything was to be home in familiar surroundings. The oncologist proceeded to tell Enid, emphatically, that she would lose her beautiful hair. This is something no young woman wants to hear, especially one who had been studying cosmetology. She was also told that her white blood cells would be closely monitored. The treatment might adversely affect and inhibit the production these cells, which the body produces to fight infection. In which case, she would have to be put on a medication called Neupogen (Filgrastim). This drug is used to help stimulate white cell production. The drug, though helpful in the production of healthy white blood cells, had its side effects. Among the side effects being skeletal pain, muscle pain, diarrhea, constipation, hair loss, headaches, fatigue, skin rashes; the list went on and on. Hopefully, she wouldn't have to take it. However, if necessary, she would have to take it and hope for the best. We prayed and believed that she would not need to take this additional drug. This drug would have to be administered by me at home; it came in injection form. I would be taught how to administer it. However, I knew that I wouldn't be able to do it if the need arose. So, I prayed that it wouldn't be necessary. My heart ached seeing my first-born child go through such pain and heartache. I just couldn't be the one to inflict yet more pain on her, besides the fact that she hated (and I use the word lightly) injections of any kind. I knew she was not about to let me near her.

Again, having heard his dire prognosis I clung onto John 11:4 "this sickness is not unto death but for the glory of God, that the Son of God might be glorified thereby..." (KJV)

Enid's first treatment went without incident. We believed that the Lord was answering our prayers. Initially, we were told that Enid had a tumor in her chest the size of half a watermelon. The tumor was wrapped around her windpipe and pressing on her heart and lungs, which explained why she was having difficulty breathing. She was in essence suffocating. We were elated when they took another soft tissue X-Ray before she left hospital and they found that the tumor had shrunk to the size of an orange. We were praising God for His faithfulness in answering our prayers.

Easter came and went, and we were grateful to the Lord for touching our daughter's life. Before Enid was released from the hospital, they inserted a port in her chest which would be used to administer the chemo she would be receiving as an outpatient in Doctor B's office.

CHAPTER 5

Enid was finally released on Monday April 4th. Though weak, she was ecstatic to be home. Tommy Franks, one of her friends from youth group, came over and coaxed her into taking a walk with him. It was a beautiful spring day, and I was so grateful for his friendship. For a moment, he helped Enid forget what she was going through and restored some sense of normalcy to her life. Though somewhat weak and tired, she went for the walk through the wooded area behind our back yard. There was a path that led to an open field; it was lush and full of life. The grass and flowers were beginning to wake after a long harsh winter. Life was in the air, birds were chirping and making nests in preparation for their new arrivals. So, it was just what Enid needed to see; life all around her and Tommy was just the person to convince to take that much needed walk.

One treatment down and five more to go. Enid was told she would lose her hair. When she took a shower, she refused to wash her hair. As I watched my daughter's beautiful hair, which once cascaded down her back, become a matted mess, I wept silently before the Lord, asking Him to give Enid the strength and courage to let it go. I knew it would grow back. She, however, was in total denial, refusing to comb it for fear of losing it.

As the days passed by, Enid began to come to grips with the fact that her hair, now totally matted, needed to be cut. Enid called me into her room and asked me to comb her hair out. This was the first time since her treatment that she had put a comb through her hair. She sat down in the chair not wanting to look in the mirror. She purposely sat facing away from the mirror. I grabbed a large Macy's bag and a brush and proceeded to gently brush out the mat which was now her hair. As I passed the brush through her hair, the entire mat of the now dead hair fell into the bag. My knees went weak as I saw what was once her beautiful hair laying in a heap in the bottom of the bag. I held back my tears as I continued with the painful task of untangling what little hair was left on Enid's head. She began to cry as I combed out her hair. Through her tears she said, "Mom, why me, why me?" There I was, a woman of prayer, a woman of faith, and all I could say to my beautiful daughter was "Honey, I don't know why." The truth was I didn't know why this was happening. However, I knew that the God I served didn't do this. I reminded her that we have an enemy, the devil. I reminded her that Jesus Himself says in John 10:10, "The thief does not come except to steal, and to kill and to destroy. I have come that they may have life and that they may have it more abundantly." (NKJV) I reminded my daughter of that scripture as often as I could. I continued to comb out Enid's hair and fill the Macy's bag with her hair. It seemed like an eternity, but finally I was finished. I took the bag, not letting her see that it was full of her once beautiful, lustrous hair, now a dull matted, lifeless heap that didn't even resemble human hair.

I came back into the room. Enid was still sitting with her back facing the mirror not wanting to look at herself. I told her that she still had some hair and that she had a really cool looking head. With a little coaxing, she finally looked in the mirror and, to my relief and surprise, handled her new look better than I had expected. Enid loved baseball hats and hats in general, so I encouraged her to get some funky hats to show off her new look. I knew she had the face for hats, so we bought some really cute hats which were just her style.

Next on our agenda was to try and find a wig that Enid would feel comfortable wearing; one which would help her feel and look more like herself. In a nearby town called Woodstown N.J., at that, time there was an American Cancer Society Resource Center. I was told they at times had wigs which were donated and were available to cancer patients free of charge. I went and looked at the wigs. Being twenty-one, I knew my daughter would think the wigs that were available at the time were too old looking for her. So, we went to several salons that carried wigs. After several failed attempts, we did find a wig that she liked, so we purchased it for her. Though it could never take the place of her beautiful hair, it was close enough to her dark brown hair coloring. Also, the length and style were similar to hers. More importantly, she was okay with it. I say okay because I can't begin to imagine how she felt losing her hair and having it replaced by a wig. She, however, was so gracious; she never complained about losing her again at least not to me any way.

Enid made one of the most painful decisions of her young life. She decided not to return to her studies in Cosmetology. That was devastating to hear. You see, she only had a couple of months to go before graduating. She was one of the top students in her class and, more importantly, she loved it. As devastated as I was, I knew she was more so. However, we fully supported her decision. She explained that the chemo caused her to become very tired and also would begin to change her appearance. She had already lost her hair and didn't want to have to explain to her classmates what she was dealing with. We understood and supported her decision because she was a beautiful young lady and was having a real difficult time dealing with all the changes taking place in her body and her life.

Three weeks passed quickly, and I needed to prepare for her next round of chemo. By preparation, I meant I had to go to the pharmacy with what looked like a booklet of prescriptions that needed to be filled. Then I would have to make an appointment with her oncologist and schedule her next treatment. As I walked into the pharmacy, located in the small shopping center five minutes from our home, and handed the booklet of prescriptions to the pharmacist, I was told that I needed to come back in an hour. They needed the time to check the insurance and fill the prescriptions. As I walked out of the pharmacy with tears in my eyes, I quietly spoke to the Lord. "Lord how are we ever going to pay for these treatments?" Then I remembered a word Terry Meeuwsen (co-host of the 700 Club TV program) had shared while I was with my daughter in the hospital. As I watched the 700 Club, Terry had a word of knowledge (this is one of the nine spiritual gifts spoken of in the Bible in 2 Corinthians, which the Lord will give to believers to share with His people.). She said, "There is a parent who is worried about medical expenses and treatments your child is going to need. God wants you to know He's got this." The word resounded in my heart and somehow, I knew that we would be okay; God had this. I returned to the pharmacy an hour later and the pharmacist handed me a shopping bag (and I do mean a shopping bag) full of drugs. I was sick to my stomach as I held my breath and waited for her to tell me what our co-pay was. She gave me back my card and said, "That will be $5.00 dollars please." I couldn't believe my ears. I handed her the $5.00 and I walked out of the pharmacy quietly weeping and thanking God for His amazing provision.

We were now in the month of April and Enid was ready for her second round of chemo. I remember Enid and I being escorted into a room where many other patients were receiving their treatments. Each one was sitting in a comfortable off-white leather recliner. They escorted Enid to one of the empty chairs and gave me a chair to sit next to her. I tried not to show any emotion as I saw them approach Enid with this huge vial that resembled a large hypodermic needle. They proceeded to slowly inject the serum from the needle into the port. At first, I could see the panic on Enid's face as they approached her. But I gently squeezed her hand and prayed with her, and she relaxed as they slowly administered the medication. We were there for approximately an hour, however, it felt like an eternity. We were happy when they finished and gave us the okay to leave. This was one of four other times we would be sitting in this room in the coming months. Now at least we knew what to expect.

Enid had somewhat adjusted to her new look and we, of course, were her biggest fans. Whenever she wore one of her funky hats, we let her know how great it looked on her, and frankly, we weren't lying. She did look great in the hats she had chosen. She had very little hair left and at times she chose not to wear the wig and wear one of her funky hats instead. At times she would even make light of her situation. I often wondered if it was for our benefit. One time, we were picking up her younger sister Jeanette from school (at Ambassador Academy in Glassboro, N.J). As she looked in the mirror, she noticed that a couple of strands of her hair were peeking out from under the brim of her hat. So, she casually reached up and instead of trying to tuck the strands back into her hat, she tugged at them, and they came loose in her fingers. She glibly looked at me and said, "This is what I love; disposable hair. If it's out of place all I have to do is pull and it's gone and you're good to go," laughing and making light of it. To which I laughed, though internally I was crying; I'm sure she was too. Enid had a way of bringing joy and laughter even into this sad situation.

It was amazing how close we had become during these last three weeks. You see we had hit a rough patch when she had turned eighteen and our relationship had become somewhat strained. However, after her diagnosis she wanted me by her side. She asked me not to leave her side. It saddened me that it took these devastating circumstances to bridge the great divide between us. Nonetheless, I loved my precious daughter, and I was committed to take her hand in mine and take this journey with her no matter what. I considered it a privilege to be asked.

Enid was doing remarkably well, though after her second treatment she developed a fever. So, we immediately took her to the hospital. To our dismay, a blood test revealed her body was not producing sufficient white blood cells and she would need to start taking the Neupogen injections. They had to be administered for ten days after her course of treatment. Again, the oncologist explained all the possible side effects, however, the alternative was worse.

Even with this setback we stood on God's Word John 11:4, "this sickness is not unto death but for the glory of God, that the Son of God might be glorified thereby..." (KJV) We left the hospital with yet another prescription and a real dilemma; "Who on earth was going to inject our daughter?" As I mentioned before, she hated, and I

45

repeat, hated shots. So naturally, I couldn't do it. Again, the thought of adding more pain to what she was already feeling was not something I relished. Yet I knew it had to be done. But who (to use a baseball analogy) would step up to the plate? Then the Lord send and angel in the form of my sister-in-law Edda. Edda graciously offered to do it. Enid was fine with the idea that her titi (a term of endearment in Spanish for aunt) was willing to do it. Enid loved her titi and knew her titi loved her and would be gentle with her. She truly was an angel sent from God at my hour of need. I will be eternally grateful for her willingness to do what I could not do. It truly was her love for Enid that enabled her to do what I couldn't do. I remember every time that Edda would leave after injecting her, Enid would sink her face into my chest and cry for just a minute. She so appreciated what Edda did, though. She just needed that cry then she would shake it off and continued her day.

I found out several years later that her titi Edda, not only came to the rescue by giving Enid her much needed injection, she spent many times with her in her hospital room. I found out that those times when I was unable to be there or had to leave Enid, she would pick up the phone and simply say to her titi, "Come." Edda would drop what she was doing, even if it meant being excused from her job at Smith Kline and she would come and spend time comforting our daughter. This is a gift of love that can never be repaid. I can only say with great humility, thank you.

May 18ᵗʰ was around the corner and our daughter Enid would be turning twenty-two. She was three months into her treatment, and we decided that we were going to live life as normally has possible. So, we decided to celebrate her birthday. After all, we had cause for celebration; our daughter was still with us, and she was fighting the good fight of faith.

We invited all our family and friends to come and celebrate with us. It was a picture-perfect day. Enid was radiant and so full of life. She had gotten used to her new look. Everyone who truly loved her was in attendance. The celebration took place in our back yard, so I had many occasions to go back into the house to retrieve something I had forgotten or needed. On one occasion I was entering the house to get some more refreshments. As I stepped into the family room from the backyard, I heard a "voice" say to me, "This will be the last birthday party you will give your daughter Enid." Being a strong woman of faith, I quickly and audibly said the following: "I rebuke you Satan, in the name of Jesus." and remembered John 11:4 "this sickness is not unto death but for the glory of God, that the Son of God might be glorified thereby..." (KJV) I got the refreshments, never telling a soul what had transpired. I enjoyed the day with our daughter, our children, Jaysen and Jeanette, and the rest of the family and friends. Enid was elated at the outpouring of love she received. It was a picture-perfect day.

Ruth Santiago

CHAPTER 6

May came and went without much incident and June was upon us. Our family and friends were exceptional. I will never forget their prayers, their help, and their acts of kindness during our daughter's illness. During one of our daughter's hospitalizations, my cousin Laura (affectionately called Tuta) got wind that our daughter Enid loved and yearned to have a napoleon (a French pastry; a blend of puff pastry and custard filling), one of her favorite desserts. So, Tuta traveled four hours by car from her home in Connecticut to bring her favorite dessert. That act of love and kindness was never forgotten by our daughter; nor by us. She couldn't believe that my cousin would do that for her; it made her feel so very loved.

As I mentioned before, Enid loved cosmetology studies, and though she had made a decision discontinue her studies, the Lord blessed her by allowing her to do what she loved most. She had several opportunities to style hair for friends and family. On one occasion one of her friends, Kristen, a high school senior living in

Bayonne New Jersey asked Enid to style her hair and do her makeup for her graduation pictures; Enid was delighted. Her friend could have easily gone to a salon, but she chose to give our daughter a chance to do what she loved. This expression of love and compassion truly blessed Enid.

The Lord also used my cousin Magda as well, by providing Enid yet another opportunity to use her craft. Magda was getting married, and she asked Enid to do her makeup and her hair. Magda had the means to use a professional hair and makeup stylist. But she chose to give Enid this honor. Enid was over the moon. This is what she loved to do, so these were some of the happiest and most fulfilling moments of her life. These acts of love and kindness done by these exceptional people helped Enid experience the Lord's love in a tangible way. It also helped distract her from what otherwise was a very sad and difficult time in her life.

June and July came and went as quickly as the other previous months. Enid was doing so well I suggested that she spend a week at Joe's parent's house in Staten Island. Enid was bored and was doing so well we thought that visiting with her grandparents and her other titis in Staten Island was just the ticket. Joe's parents and titis adored Enid and would relish the idea of having her spend quality time with them. Enid had finished her chemo for the month and was feeling quite well and looking forward to seeing her family. So, she packed her bag and off we went. Staten Island is two hours away from our home, a drive we did not mind taking if it meant that our daughter was going to have some much-needed fun and distraction.

Two days into her visit, around 9:00 p.m. in the evening, we got a call from Enid. She informed us that she had a slight fever. Hearing the concern in her voice, Joe and I got dressed quickly. My mom was living next door with my brother and his family. We asked mom to come over and stay with Jaysen and Jeanette. We headed back to Staten Island, arrived around 11:30 p.m. and immediately drove back home with Enid. We took her directly to Underwood Memorial hospital to be checked. She was taken into a cubicle to be examined. As a precaution, blood was drawn immediately in order to determine if she was producing the proper amount of white blood cells needed to fight any infection or cold, she might be experiencing. To our delight, she was fine, so they sent us home. We arrived at home around four in the morning, exhausted, we dropped into bed and fell fast asleep. Around nine o'clock in the morning, I felt a body on top of me. When I opened my eyes, it was my daughter Enid staring into my blood shot eyes with a big silly grin. She said "Mom, take me back to Staten Island. I want to spend the rest of the week with my grandma Lydia and grandpa Jose and my titi's." Exhausted as we were, once again, we got dressed and this time we weren't going to pick Enid up, we were taking her back to finish her stay with her family, at her own request. She had a wonderful time with her grandparents and titi's and made wonderful memories. They were eternally grateful to have Enid back.

During our daughter's illness I was the youth pastor at our church at Beckett Assembly of God. All the youth I ministered to had been cheering Enid on and standing in faith with us that Enid would have the victory. They sent cards and videos encouraging her to continue to believe for her miracle. She got cards and books and an outpouring of love from all who knew her. She was so grateful for the overwhelming expressions of love she received.

CHAPTER 7

Her last treatment was finished and other than some joint pain, Enid was doing fabulously. We were now scheduled to have her last bone scan which would show how the treatment had eradicated the cancer from her body. We went to what was then called Booth Radiology, to get the bone scan. They gave us the X-Rays to take to the oncologist to be read to us. After the scan, Enid and I went to lunch at Friendly's restaurant. Enid couldn't wait to see the oncologist for the results, so she took the X-Ray out and looked at them. Being a soft tissue X-Ray, the rays by-pass the bones and shows any abnormalities. As we looked, we could see what appeared to be a small mass; too small to make out. She looked at me and naturally, I couldn't decipher what was showing up in the X-Ray. However, I felt in my heart that it wasn't good. I tried not to show my concern. When we got home, we made an appointment with the oncologist for the very next day; luckily, he had an opening.

He looked at the X-Ray and said it looked like residual left over from the tumor. However, since Enid continued to experience skeletal pain, he felt it best to do a bone marrow aspiration. A sample of her bone marrow would be taken to make sure the cancer had not spread to her bone marrow. Both Enid and I were in shock. *This nightmare was supposed to be over. What is going on?* I thought. We had no choice but to agree. We needed to know what was going on.

Enid was admitted the day before my birthday, August 24th. They did the bone marrow aspiration that morning. We were told that we would have the results the next day. I let Joe know what was happening and he came to the hospital that evening straight from work. Once again, as before, Enid buried her head in her father's chest and wept. I stood numbly by as I watched our daughter's life once again hanging in the balance. I couldn't wrap my brain around what was happening. Still, I clung to the Word God had given me months earlier; John 11:4, "this sickness is not unto death but for the glory of God, that the Son of God might be glorified thereby..." **(KJV)**

I spent the evening with her trying to comfort her and praying for a birthday miracle. Enid slept on and off through the night waiting with anticipation for the results of the test. I took a moment along with Joe to step out of the room. Joe had come home so we could hear the results of the tests together. As I saw the oncologist walking down the hall towards us, we saw another doctor with him which we had not seem before. My knees weakened and I felt as though I would faint. Within my heart I knew that this doctor meant that the news was not good.

The oncologist's look on his face said it all. He was very gentle in his delivery but none the less it was like a bolt had hit my heart when he proceeded to inform us that the cancer had spread to our daughter's bones. She needed a bone marrow transplant. It was the only other course of treatment available. We were stunned. He excused himself and went into our daughter's room to give her the news. She began to sob as Joe held her. We assured her that it wasn't over, that we had a God who was bigger than lymphoma. We also reminded her of the word I had received from the Lord., John 11:4, "this sickness is not unto death but for the glory of God, that the Son of God might be glorified thereby..." (KJV) This seemed to bring Enid some comfort. We held each other and prayed.

The next day we were assigned a new General Practitioner. We had informed the hospital that we were not happy with the current doctor and requested a change. The following morning, as I stood in the hall, I saw this larger-than-life doctor approaching me. He introduced himself. I'll call him Dr. C. He looked like he was totally out of his element, but his kind and gentle demeanor won us over. He became our primary physician and still is to this day. This gentle giant shared how very sorry he was for all that we were going through and pledged to be there for us every step of the way; that he would do his best to answer any questions we had. That brought some comfort to both Joe and I because we were at a loss as to where go from there.

The oncologist explained to us what needed to take

place. Enid needed a bone marrow transplant. The cancer had spread to her bone marrow and that was the cause of her skeletal pain. He explained the severity of the situation. Once again, our world was turned upside down. We couldn't wrap our minds around what the oncologist was saying. "No! No! No! this couldn't be happening." Yet it was. There on the hospital bed sat our beautiful twenty-two-year-old daughter near hysteria as she too was having a hard time wrapping her head around what the oncologist was saying. He explained that this was our only option. There was nothing more that could be done. The cancer was very aggressively moving into the bone marrow and would continue to ravage Enid's body if we didn't act quickly. In essence, what he was saying was that we were in a race to save her live. Enid agreed to proceed (we say, Enid agreed, because though we were her parents, she was an adult, so the decision to proceed had to come from her) with the only course of treatment available to her. The oncologist left the room and we just put our arms around our daughter and wept.

I mustered enough strength and faith, along with Joe, to remind her of the word the Lord had given me at the very beginning of this trial; found in John 11:4: "this sickness is not unto death but for the glory of God, that the Son of God might be glorified thereby..." (KJV) How? We had no clue, but the scripture gave us peace and an assurance that we were not alone in this battle. The Lord was very present, and it was evident to all who knew us. Even the nursing staff were in awe of the peace we had in the midst of the direst of circumstances. Yes, we cried and were saddened by the turn of events, however, the presence of the Lord was evident. We were reminded that our faith would be tested, not might, but would be tested; we read the following in 1st Peter 1:7 -- "that the trial of your faith, being much more precious than of gold that perisheth, though it be tried with fire, might be found unto praise and honor and glory at the appearing of Jesus Christ" (KJV). We were being tested in a way that we wouldn't wish on our worst enemy. Nonetheless, though our faith was being put through the fire, we knew that the Lord was right there with us just as He was with the three Jewish boys Meshach, Shadrach, and Abednego in the book of Daniel 3:16-28. They were thrown in the fire for not bowing down to an idol, yet in the midst of the fire, Jesus showed up and they were delivered.

Just to be clear: we don't believe that this sickness was brought about by God but by the devil .... Jesus said: "in this world you will have tribulations..." John 16:33; (KJV) and: "the thief cometh not but to steal and to kill and to destroy" John 10:10 (KJV). Joe, Enid, and I were believing that Jesus was right along with us in the midst of this fiery trial. We weren't alone and the peace the nursing staff saw was that confidence that we placed in a loving God who was watching over us.

This peace that the Lord gave us translated to the Lord giving me many opportunities to, not only share our faith with some of the nursing staff but on one occasion, to pray with a patient who was undergoing surgery the next day.

She had just happened to be admitted into our daughter's room the night before we got the harrowing news that Enid would need a bone marrow transplant. This young woman was crying and very frightened. I went over to her and asked her if I could pray for her; she agreed, and we prayed. The peace of the Lord came upon her, and she slept through the night. The following day she had her surgery, and all went well. The nursing staff noticed how we were sensitive to other peoples' needs and it opened the door for me to share the hope we had in Christ. In spite of the difficulty we were facing, I was thankful to be used of God to comfort others in need.

Our oncologist made arrangements for our daughter to be transferred from Underwood Memorial Hospital to Cooper Hospital in Camden, NJ, where the search for a bone marrow donor would begin. They transferred Enid to a private room in Underwood while we waited to be transferred. They wanted Enid to be comfortable and were sensitive to the need to keep Enid free from any other complication which would delay the transplant.

CHAPTER 8

While we waited to be transferred, I had an opportunity to speak to Enid. I told her that we were praying and believing God for her miracle, but that she needed to put her trust totally in Him. I said to her that if she was holding anything back, now was the time to surrender it to the Lord; to allow the Lord to search her heart and if there was any bitterness or unforgiveness, she needed to let it all go and allow Him to totally cleanse her. I reminded her that He was there, ready to take her hand in His and walk with her through this horrific time in her life. I assured her that as her parents we could pray and seek God for her, but this time this was a battle that she had to fight; we couldn't fight it for her. I told her that I was going to step out of the room to give her a little quiet time alone.

I remember leaving the room and going to the window. We were on the 5th floor and Enid's room was a stone's throw away from the window. I stood looking out the window praying and crying quietly before the Lord, "Walk with her Lord, guide her and comfort her. Lord, let her sense your presence and Lord, strengthen this mother's heart that has been, once again, shattered into a million pieces. Give me the strength to be there for Enid through this journey which has been chosen for her to travel. Help me to cry with her, to laugh with her, to know when to speak and when not to speak. Let me be a blessing to my daughter. That she may not only see a mother's love, but Your love as well."

I composed myself, wiped the tears from my eyes and quietly headed back to Enid's room. As I peeked in, Enid was on her knees quietly with her head bowed (she was now completely bald as the treatments had totally caused her to lose what little hair she had left,) praying to the Lord. I waited a while before I walked back into room giving her the time she needed to spend before her Lord. Looking in again I noticed she was now sitting in the chair alongside her bed. I quietly walked back into the room never letting her know what I had witnessed. It was such a sacred moment between her and her Savior that I felt I had no right to say anything.

We were finally transferred to Cooper Hospital in Camden. Once at Cooper Hospital we met with the oncologist who would take over our daughter's care. He told us that Enid couldn't be put on the National Bone Marrow Donor Transplant List because she was in dire need of a transplant and time was of the essence. Our best option was our immediate family. They would be tested and hopefully one would be a match. As the oncologist explained, I was devastated because I knew that I was automatically disqualified because during my pregnancy with Enid I had gotten hepatitis D, so I could never be a blood donor, let alone give my bone marrow. As a mother, wanting to give my life if need be for my child; My hands were tied, so I prayed that someone in our immediate family would be a match.

Our son Jaysen was tested and found to be a compatible match. Jaysen was only seventeen years old at the time, but he was more than willing to have the procedure if it meant helping save his older sister's life, whom he adored. This procedure was not very comfortable for the person who would be donating the marrow and not without any risk. Our son would be anesthetized, a needle would then be inserted into the rear pelvic bone where a large quantity of bone marrow is located. The bone marrow would then be extracted. Several skin and bone punctures would be required to extract sufficient bone marrow for the transplant. Yet he was undaunted and was willing do whatever it took to give his sister a chance to live.

Enid had to undergo many tests before being admitted into the transplant unit. They wanted to ensure that her body would be able to handle the treatment that she was about to receive. They had to check her lungs, her heart, her liver and other organs to make sure they were not compromised. One night while we were resting after a battery of tests, we were settling down for the night and I felt I just had to ask her a question. "Enid," I said, "are you angry with God?" She quickly responded, "Oh no, mom." She went on to say, "Mom, that would be like sending an innocent man to the electric chair. I'm angry at the devil. If he were here right now, I'd give him a swift kick in the pants" (not exactly her words). I knew then that Enid truly understood that the God she served hadn't done this to her. That gave me great peace knowing she truly understood who her enemy was; it wasn't the Lord; it was the devil.

On several occasions, I needed to get home to bathe and check in on Jeanette and Jaysen. The guilt at times overwhelmed me. I was committed to being with our oldest daughter, but I also had two other children at home who also needed me; so, I was conflicted. I wished at times that I could split myself in two so that I could be with all of them. As I drove home this particular day, I hit rock bottom. I was crying inconsolably. My tears were blinding me, and I was having difficulty seeing. As I cried, a song came on the radio: "Praise the Lord." As I listened to the words through my tears, I was reminded that as I praised the Lord the chains that bound me would fall. They would have no power over me, over the pain that I was feeling.

As I sang, it was as if the Lord Himself filled the car with His presence and I began to sense a peace that I so desperately needed; as well as renewed strength. Things hadn't changed, but I had. I knew that I wasn't alone. I got home. Thankfully, my family had taken over during the times when I couldn't be with Jeanette and Jaysen and they were okay. I say, okay, because deep in my heart I knew they, too, were hurting. I returned to the hospital refreshed and ready to face whatever came next.

As I said before, Enid went through a battery of tests in preparation for the impending bone marrow transplant. On one occasion they were doing an ultrasound of her organs and having promised that I would be present at all her tests, I held her hand while the ultrasound technician ran the probe over her stomach. Enid fixed her gaze on me and not the screen, watching and waiting to see my reaction as the probe went from organ to organ. I looked straight into the screen hoping she would not detect my disbelief as I saw mass upon mass on each of the organs scanned. Every time the technician saw a mass, she took a picture. All I could hear was the clicking sound of the camera as picture after picture was being taken. I knew that every click, every picture represented a mass. I was having difficulty breathing; I thought I would collapse. I mustered all the strength I needed as I held Enid's hand and lovingly told her she would be okay.

When the scan was finally over and they were getting ready to wheel her to her room, I bent down and kissed her forehead and told her that I was going to the lobby to get some coffee. My diet consisted, those days, of large cups of coffee, which I would sometimes nurse for days. I quickly took the elevator down to the lobby. As I stepped out of the elevator, I decided coffee could wait. I needed time in the Chapel with the Lord. He had given me a word at the very beginning, and I continued to hold unto that word- John 11:4, "this sickness is not unto death but for the glory of God, that the Son of God might be glorified thereby..." (KJV). I just needed time alone with the Lord. I needed the comfort that can only come from being in His presence. I needed Abba Father to wrap His loving arms around me and just hold me. I laid prostrate on the floor, not giving any thought to whether the floor was clean or not. That was the last thing on my mind. I wanted to humble myself before the Lord. I wanted to ask the Lord to spare my child. I knew from what I had seen on the ultrasound that my baby was at death's door. Only a miracle from God could save her. I knew He was more than capable of healing her because you see I am a miracle myself.

As an infant living in Lares, Puerto Rico during the 50's, I was an acute asthmatic. Because of circumstances beyond my mother's control, she was forced to leave us with our grandmother while she tried to make a life in the States and eventually send for us. She, however, did not know that I was suffering from asthma. The asthma attacks I had were so severe that many times my grandmother would be forced to take me to the town clinic. During my last visit to the clinic, they told her to take me home, make me comfortable because I was going to die.

My grandmother couldn't read or write but she was a woman of faith. She laid me on the bed and prayed over me committing me to the Lord. Years later she told me that she asked the Lord to heal me or take me home; that she couldn't bear to see me suffer another asthma attack. She went out to the yard and slaughtered a chicken and made a broth for me. She told me that I had been unable to eat anything, but she believed that the God she prayed to would heal me. So, by faith, she prepared the broth for me. I made it through the night and for the first time in days I was able to hold something in my stomach. The rest is history as they say! I was healed.

So, as I prayed, I remembered that, and with renewed faith I went to the Lord. I knew that if He could heal me as an infant when I was sent home to die, He could heal my daughter as well. I prayed and cried and begged and pleaded. I even tried to bargain with Him. I asked Him to take my life in her place. I told Him whatever He wanted from me, all He had to do was just ask. I'd do anything, go anywhere He wanted; "Just Lord, please heal Enid. Lord, heal my child." As I prayed and cried, I heard an audible voice say these words; "It is finished." I couldn't believe my ears. I remember saying, "Lord, 'it is finished'? What do you mean?"

In my heart of hearts, I knew what He was saying. The reason I knew what He was saying to me was because several weeks prior to Enid being readmitted into the hospital, before being re-diagnosed, I had been praying in the living room with my mom. And as I prayed, I had a vision of an angel scooping Enid into his arms and swiftly taking her up to heaven. But as I prayed, waiting for him to bring her back, the vision faded, and she was never returned to her bed. I never told a soul because I was holding on to the word the Lord had given me- John 11:4 "this sickness is not unto death but for the glory of God, that the Son of God might be glorified thereby..." (KJV) As I heard God's audible voice once again; those words

"It is finished," I knew, for the first time since Enid had been diagnosed, I felt that the Lord might be going to take Enid home. I remember how I felt: I cried; I screamed; then I remembered the promise. I had made a promise to the Lord many years ago that I would serve Him no matter what. I didn't know what "no matter what" really meant at the time. Why would I say that to the Lord? Because you see, He saved me radically. I was so lost without hope. He not only saved me, but shortly after I got saved, at around two o'clock in the morning, the Holy Spirit filled my room with His tangible presence. He called me by my name. I heard the Lord say, "Ruth, Ruth, arise." As I arose, the room was filled with the presence of the Holy Spirit, and for two hours I was bathed in a love that words fail to adequately describe. I knew it was the Lord's presence. as I quietly sat in awe, the Holy Spirit read to me from the book of Matthew Chapter 6. To this day, every time I speak about this encounter, I can't contain my tears. That God would stop time and eternity to speak to me was more than I could ever hope for or deserve, yet He did. That is why I said and continue to say, "I will serve You no matter what."

After this encounter, I chose to believe that "it is finished," meant that Enid would be healed. That our prayers had been answered; no more prayers were needed. It was done. Enid would have the victory. Why did I choose to believe that she would recover? Remember I had received a word from the Lord in the very beginning and I chose to stand upon that word. John 11:4 "this sickness is not unto death but for the glory of God, that the Son of God might be glorified thereby..." (KJV)

I couldn't tell my family what had transpired in the chapel. I kept it to myself. I got up from my prostrate position, dusted myself off, wiped my eyes and chose to dismiss the encounter. I headed back to my daughter's room. I continued to stand on the Word of God. I just kept repeating the Scripture in my head; John 11:4- "this sickness is not unto death but for the glory of God, that the Son of God might be glorified thereby...", (KJV) over and over again, still refusing to believe what I had heard and choosing to believe life for my daughter in spite of what my heart was telling me. I remembered what the word of God says in Numbers 23:19; "God is not a man that He should lie." I had received a word and I chose not to be moved.

CHAPTER 9

The week before the transplant was scheduled, Enid made a special request. She asked to be allowed to go home for the weekend. Joe and I spoke with the doctors, and they were opposed. They were concerned that Enid might get a cold and delay the transplant. Upon Enid's insistence, they relented and allowed us to take our daughter home; that was Friday, October 28th. The months had flown by since her second diagnosis. Enid had spent most of time in and out of the hospital during this time. One thing that saddened her was the fact that her friends stayed away. She told me in the language of her peers, that her friends had "dissed" her, (her words, not mine) but I understood what she was saying. She felt alone and I didn't have words of comfort; only to say that maybe it was too hard for them to see her this way. With that she replied, "but mom, they were supposed to be my friends".

Enid was so looking forward to a weekend at home. Having gotten permission to take her home for the weekend, we bundled her up making sure she wouldn't get a draft that would result in a postponement of the procedure. Once home, Enid spent most of her time in her bedroom. She didn't have much energy and preferred to spend her time in the room she loved so much. One evening, as I passed her room to go and check on her, she called me in and asked if I would lay beside her. I climbed into bed with her, and she snuggled against my chest with her back nestled against me and asked me to hold her. I took my baby in my arms and held her close to me. She was totally bald, not a hair was left on her beautiful head, but to me she was the most beautiful girl in the world. I held back the tears as we snuggled together for what seemed an eternity. I prayed with her and held her till she fell asleep. I got out of the bed quietly and went to my bedroom to try and sleep; the next day would be Sunday and Enid wanted to go to church. Enid rose Sunday morning and was very weak, but she insisted on going to church. I went into her room to help her get dressed. I got her wig, but this time she decided that she would not wear it. She also decided that she wouldn't wear any makeup either. She just put on one of her funky hats.

We all got in the car and went off to church. When we got there, she insisted on sitting in the back of the sanctuary with the youth. We helped Enid to her seat and Joe, and I went and sat in the back of the sanctuary near the sound system which was on the right. We were in the middle of the worship service when I glanced over to where Enid was seated. We saw our daughter, with great difficulty, rise from her chair and begin to make her way to the front. She was so unstable that I quickly rose to my feet to go and help her make her way to the front of the sanctuary. As I started in her direction, the Lord stopped me dead in my tracks. I heard Him say to me, "Ruth let her go, she is coming to Me."

I sat back down with tears streaming down my face. I watched helplessly as my baby girl struggled to make it to the altar. Enid knelt before her Lord and all the youth that were present that Sunday morning went to the front of the sanctuary and knelt beside her. They crowded next to her and wrapped their arms around her and prayed and cried together. It was such a sacred moment, we never talked about it. The service ended and Enid struggled to get back to the car. Tommy Franks came along side of her and help her to the car. As the day ended, we all went to bed knowing that the next day, Monday morning, we would be returning Enid back to Cooper Hospital to begin preparations for the Bone Marrow Transplant.

When we arrived at the hospital, they were waiting for her. Enid was admitted into the Transplant unit. Unlike the rooms she had been in at Underwood, which were very drab and depressing, the room in this wing of Cooper Hospital was bright and colorful and very comfortable. It was a change of pace from what we had experienced thus far, and I was so grateful. It was bad enough that she would be in isolation for a month but imagine being in room that was drab and institutional looking. This room had large windows overlooking the heliport where the helicopters would land and take off. This activity afforded us some distraction as we watched the helicopters land and take off from time to time. Sometimes, when I saw a helicopter lift off the ground, for a brief moment I would imagine that Enid and I would be flying off to some tropical destination, where she would be sitting on a sandy beach, her toes digging into the sand as the wind blew through her beautiful hair; and she was whole and well. Then the phone would ring, or a doctor would walk in. then I would snap out of it to find myself in what was our harsh reality, a reality I wouldn't wish on any parent or child. As I came back to reality, I was so thankful that the GOD I serve is a GOD who was and is more than capable of keeping me in HIS perfect peace, as long as my mind and heart was fixed on HIM. I chose to stay focused on HIM and HIS promise, John 11:4 "this sickness is not unto death but for the glory of God, that the Son of God might be glorified thereby..." (KJV)

My mom, Amparo, was having a very difficult time seeing her first-born grandchild fighting for her life. But she loved her, so she decided to come to see her. While Enid was in isolation, family members were allowed limited visits. Naturally, they had to be healthy in order to prevent Enid from contracting any sickness. Even a cold could prove to be dangerous to her health as her immune system was very compromised. In order to visit, all who entered her room had to wear a sterile gown and a mask. Thankfully, the Lord gave my mom the strength to see Enid and not fall apart. Enid adored her grandmother and was elated to see her. The visit was brief, but it blessed both my mom and my daughter. After the visit, I spoke to mom and she told me that when she looked at Enid, she saw her with a full head of hair and looking beautiful. I believe the Lord allowed my mom to see Enid whole and well; it was His gift to her.

Enid, as I said before, was totally bald. The medicine caused her face to become swollen and had what is called a "moon" face. This is typical of people who are undergoing chemo. She was retaining fluids and looked swollen, her tiny figure was now hidden under all the excess water weight she was gaining. The chemo treatment Enid was undergoing was designed to kill the diseased cells and malfunctioning bone marrow. The process is called conditioning. It consists of high doses of chemo that would destroy all of Enid's bone marrow in order to prepare room for the new cells (called stem cells) to grow and take the place of the affected bone marrow. Once the process was completed, Enid would have to rest for three days after which the new cells would be introduced to her body by way of a central venous catheter.

Enid had entered the transplant phase and was having a very difficult time with what she was told of how the process was to proceed. The transplant was now scheduled for November 2nd. Joe and I slipped out of the room and went down to the chapel to pray. Joe was brokenhearted over what Enid was going through. Through his tears, he shared his father's heart with me. He told me that he couldn't stand to see our daughter suffer this way. He felt we needed to release her; to let her know that if she wanted to go home with the Lord, it was okay. As we cried and prayed together, we both agreed to do it.

CHAPTER 10

The preparation was brutal; they gave Enid a cocktail of pills that could choke a horse. I was allowed to stay with her, 24/7. I slept in a chair that opened into a small bed; not that I was getting much sleep.

On Tuesday, Enid took a turn for the worse. The oncologist came and spoke with us. He took my hand in his and told me that they were going to postpone the transplant because Enid was having a hard time handling the prep. Then he asked, if our daughter expired would we want to have her revived. I looked him squarely in his eyes and said, "our daughter belongs to the Lord. He, and only He, will decide whether she goes home to be with Him or she stays here with us. She has fought a valiant fight and we have committed her to the Lord." The oncologist made his apologies and left. I went into the room where our daughter was lying. By this time, she knew what the oncologist had decided. She was so very sick and was having difficulty breathing. We stood by her side; we had no words; what could we say!

Joe and I stayed up most of the night by her side, holding her hand and praying for John 11:4 "this sickness is not unto death but for the glory of God, that the Son of God might be glorified thereby..." (KJV) to be fulfilled in our daughter's life. The transplant that had been scheduled for Wednesday, the very next day, now had been postponed. Having had a really rough night the previous night, I sat on the recliner which had been my bed since entering the transplant unit. I was exhausted and, for what I thought was a moment, I closed my eyes. I woke up startled. Joe was sitting next to Enid with her hand clasped in his. I knew I needed to speak the words no parent would ever want to say to his child. I needed to allow her the freedom to choose, whether to stay and continue the fight, or go home with her Lord. I rose from the recliner and took her hand. Joe was standing on the left side of the bed; I was on the right. As I held her hand, I told her, "Enid, if you want to go home with the Lord, it's okay." As I spoke those words, she took one last deep breath and a single tear trickled down her right cheek as she entered into eternity.

On November 2nd 1994, our precious daughter slipped into eternity. Standing at her bedside, it was if the glory of the Lord filled that room and a peace like I had never felt in my life filled our hearts. I looked at our child and before our eyes she was transformed back to her natural weight. You see, she had become so bloated that she had looked nothing like herself. The Lord was so very gracious and restored her to her natural weight. Her skin looked radiant, and she looked like she was sleeping peacefully.

We called for the nurse, who came in quickly and examined her. She confirmed that Enid was gone. She was so very tender with us as she told us how sorry she was for our loss. The Lord gave us the strength to pack all our daughter's belongings. As the nurse was about to leave the room, I remembered that there was a particular plaque in the room with the scripture found in Philippians 4:13 which says, "I can do all things through Christ who strengthens me," which she had admired. I took it off the wall and I gave it to her. She hugged me and quietly left the room, giving us time alone with our beautiful twenty-two-year-old daughter. We lingered for a little while and kissed our beautiful daughter one last time and quietly left the hospital.

CHAPTER 11

I know now, more than ever before, that it was God's strength and His keeping grace that helped us to leave that hospital, leaving our daughter there. It was as if He enveloped both Joe and I in HIS loving arms and carried us through the long corridors of that hospital with the understanding that that would be the last time we would see our daughter again on this side of eternity, but with the assurance that someday we would be reunited for all eternity. As we left Enid there, we both knew she had had the victory over cancer. You see the cancer didn't have the victory; we knew that our daughter had gone to be with the Lord where no disease could ever touch her again. That cancer that had ravished her body had to be banished back to the pit of hell where it came from.

We left the hospital and arrived at our home only to find that my mom was waiting for us. As we entered the living room, we told her that Enid had gone home to be with the Lord. Needless to say, my mom didn't handle the news well and had to be given a tranquilizer to calm her down. My brother Nelson, a pastor, a man of God, and a man of faith, was inconsolable. After making sure our mom was okay, he went out to the woods behind our home to weep before the Lord. Like all of us, he questioned God. As He cried and prayed, the Lord gave him a vision of Enid. Enid was standing at Heaven's door. She turned for an instant and he said it looked like she had a tear in her eye. She waved, turned back and the doors of Heaven were opened, and she went in. This vision gave my brother Nelson a tremendous sense of peace. As he shared his vision with us, he had no way of knowing that our daughter had one tear streaming down her left cheek as she slipped into eternity. So, we knew, without a doubt, that the vision was from the Lord.

Later, my brother wrote the following poem in our daughter's memory, birthed from his pain.

How Long Must I Wait

Dedicated to the Loving Memory of Enid Santiago
who died of non-Hodgkin's Lymphoma 1994.

How long must I wait, when the pain seems endless?
How long must I wait when the trials seem relentless?
How long must when the cupboard is bare, when the oil and the
flour and the money are scarce?
How long must I wait when the illness grows stronger, and there's
no cure insight?
When the light turns to darkness and the day turns to night?
How long must I wait?
Yet in all of these trials, In the eye of the storm, there is a
voice that I hear far, yet gentile and warm.
And that voice says to me with assurance unshaken, "Your prayers
will be answered, your faith is not mistaken."
Though others have chosen to turn down the road, though they've
carried their burdens, though they've kept their own load.
I say to you my servant, "Keep the faith do not fear, For I the Lord
Jesus shall dry all your tears.
And all of your pain and all of your sorrow, shall soon turn to joy,
in a bit, yes tomorrow.
So when the battles grow stronger, when the storm rages on!
When you can go no further and all in life's going wrong!
Remember these words
"How Long Must I Wait"
"Till Heavens Doors Open and You Go Through God's Gates"
Leonard N. Santiago

The next couple of days were like a blur. Both Joe
and I clung to our Lord for we knew that only He could
help us get through the next agonizing days. We had
funeral arrangements to make, family to call and all the
other details which were necessary to bury our precious
daughter Enid. This was all very new to us. We had never
buried a child, However, the Lord in His infinite mercy
walked with us through this difficult time. He brought to
us precious friends and family, as well as church family,
to help us get through this difficult time of deep sorrow.

CHAPTER 12

My husband and I went to the Daley Funeral home in downtown Swedesboro. Mrs. Daley, the owner, walked us through the process and helped make what was a horrendous situation somewhat bearable. Like any mother with a daughter, I had dreamed that one day I would be buying my daughter Enid's wedding gown. Instead, I had to now shop for the dress she would be buried in. To say that this was heart wrenching is an understatement; but once again the Lord was ever present to encircle me in His love, His peace, and His strength. It was the hardest purchase I ever made.

Mrs. Daley did a wonderful job with our daughter. Enid looked like a beautiful young bride. Her dress was ecru with some lace; it was very simple, but elegant. I remember standing there in front of my daughter's coffin, numb with pain. I couldn't cry. Many mistook my demeanor for callousness. What people didn't know or understood was that I had chosen to allow the Lord to carry me through this horrendously painful time in my life. Had it not been for HIS amazing grace, I would've lost my mind the very first day Enid had been diagnosed. I chose, however, to allow the Lord to carry me and He did just that. I knew tears would come, but for at this moment in time the Lord was my peace.

Many showed up to pay their respects, family, and friends alike. Some were still in a state of shock, not wanting to believe that a God of love could allow someone so young to die. I found myself at times comforting others rather than being comforted myself. Again, all I can say, that it was the Lord in me. I take no glory; He gets all the glory. I remember during one of the viewings at Daley Funeral Home, that I was asked why I wasn't angry with God; after all He could have healed her, and He hadn't. At the moment the question was posed, all I could do was smile and walk away. I didn't have the energy to defend or explain God's decision. All I knew was that He loved me, and He would help me understand in due time. I had to trust in Him and His unfailing love.

Our daughter would be buried that coming Saturday. Joe and I wanted to lay to rest our daughter's remains as soon as possible. The idea of having her body in a cold impersonal morgue any longer than necessary, caused us more pain than we could bear.

When our daughter was eighteen years old, like most teenagers, she had wanted someone special in her life. Knowing this, I wrote her the following poem to encourage her.

The Love of Christ

When love begins to bloom and grow
It's fragrant like the brightest rose.
But
As the rose which fades and dies,
So often so does love.
There is a love that never dies,
Whose fragrance never fades.
It is the Love of Jesus Christ
Which beckons you today.

Written by Ruth Santiago

When I wrote this, I wrote it to encourage her to seek the love of Jesus first and He would send someone special into her life at the appropriate time. Little did I know that this poem would be used as part of the bulletin for her funeral service. Lucy, our church secretary, felt it would be an appropriate addition to her memorial bulletin. Truer words had never been spoken. Jesus loved her and had beckoned her to His side.

Saturday came quickly and all who loved Enid, both friends and family, were present to say good-bye to a young woman who had graced us with her presence for such a short time and who was loved so greatly. The funeral service was beautiful. Many participated; songs were sung; the eulogy was read. Frankly, I don't remember much of what went on during the service. I do remember, however, that a brother in our church named Chris Moyer asked if he could sing a song during the service in honor of our daughter. Little did Chris know that the song he picked to sing, The Lord is My Shepherd, which comes from Psalms 23, was our daughter's favorite verses in the Bible. Chris sung that song with such an anointing; I know everyone present was touched and blessed.

I was still in shock. Truth be told, I was just going through the motions, doing what I knew needed to be done. I do remember, however, the day of the burial. It was Saturday November 5th 1994. It was an Indian Summer. All the leaves had fallen from the trees, but it was warm and sunny. I knew I was being cradled in the arms of my Savior. I knew that the Lord was carrying us all, as Joe, Jaysen, Jeanette and I stood beside our daughter's grave to say our good-byes. Pastor Petrucci, our pastor at the time, spoke some final words. Flowers were laid on her coffin as a final goodbye and a sign of condolence. Then people quietly left the side of the grave. Physically, I was there, but a part of my heart was buried alongside my daughter that beautiful Indian Summer Day. I couldn't cry as I said my good-byes to my precious child. I knew that if I began to cry, I would never be able to stop. Once again those who saw me might have thought, *how callous*. But it wasn't that I was unfeeling, it was that the Holy Spirit had strengthened me to go through what I was going through at that moment.

As I left my daughter's gravesite, I heard God's still

small voice say to me "I have kept you in My perfect peace, did I not? You never reverted to drinking or smoking to get you through. Instead, you placed your hand in mine and haven't I been faithful?" I whispered under my breath, "Yes Lord, you have." You see the former me, without Christ in my life, would've definitely reverted to my former ways of drinking or smoking or to asking for some form of tranquilizer to help me get through this horrendous time. But my Lord gave me His Comforter to guide and strengthen me. He was keeping me in perfect peace as long as I stayed connected to Him. Again, I heard the Lord say to me, "I answered your prayers; she served Me until the day I took her home." As He spoke, my mind raced to the many times, with tears in my eyes, I would be in the kitchen cleaning the stove and crying for my children. My prayer was always the same. "Lord, I don't want fame and riches for my children; all I want is that they love You with their whole heart." I knew that if they first loved the Lord, if they put Him first in their lives, everything else would fall into place. Here at my daughter's burial, the Lord reminded me of that prayer and how He had answered it. So how could I be angry at a God who had heard and answered my prayer?

CHAPTER 13

Several days after our daughter passed away, I got the following letter in the mail dated November 9th 1994. It so touched my heart that I felt it necessary to include it here:

November 9, 1994

Robin Wiker
412 Greenview Dr.
Turnersville, NJ
08012

Dear Brother & Sister Santiago,

I extend my heart full of compassion and love during this time. God is mighty in all things. We may not always like some of the things that happen. He has completed a greater work, than we can sometimes understand. God used the both of you to create a glorious work in Enid. A young woman beautiful on the outside, and the inside. I praise God for the opportunity to have met you and your family. What an example of a Godly family.

Even though I knew Enid for a brief time, it was precious. The light and breath of Christ was upon her. We know in Christ she was victorious even over death. I want to share something with you. Last Wednesday when we were praying in one accord, God showed me something. He gave me a peace before I left. In my spirit and experience there was not much time left.

I glanced out the window and saw the thick airy multitude of cloud hanging.

God quickened it to my spirit that He was
bring the heavens to her. I knew the angels
were about interceding for that time of
ascension. The enemy may have thought he
won, wrong.

I know how difficult it is to loose
someone so close. I lost my sister 6 years
ago to cancer. I know your pain, and joy.
Leaving go of someone you love is agony at
times. While they are sick, you live, sleep,
and think about it. The joy is knowing they
are removed from the situation, and are in
the presence of God. That is something we
all strive for.

As a body of believers, we will
continue to lift up your family in prayer. I
know God's love, grace, mercy, and peace
will fill you. Enid's life is still a living
testimony to others. Christ's light from
within her touched so many. May God's
word minister to you.

1 John 5:4 For whatever is born of
God overcomes the world. And this is the
victory that has overcome the world - our
faith.

May the Lord Jesus Christ minister
through and to you during this time. Please
know what a blessing and an
encouragement you have been to me.

All Christ's Love & Mine

Robin

I am an avid journaler. I love to put my thoughts into words. It became a form of release for me during that time. Several days after receiving the above letter, I penned my last entry in the journal I was keeping during our daughter's illness. I'd like to share with you my final entry eight days after my daughter went home to be with the Lord:

Ruth Santiago

11/10/94

All that I've written in the pages
before this one seems a hundred years ago.
I'm still uncertain whether we've
been dreaming. I can't grasp the
reality of our loss.

Cnd was our first born. She was
pampered and loved from the day she
was born.

She was not only loved by us her
mom and dad. She was loved by
all who knew her. Her life had worth
she was never hateful at least not that
I ever saw. I guess I had a blind spot
when it came to her.

I really believed that You were going
to send her here on to earth. When
I think about her entire life. She

95

I wasn't really to any different than your typical young person.

She loved life. She struggled to live up to the standards she felt we placed upon her. Yet she loved the family passionately. She was witty and she could be profound, but mostly she was very simple and uncomplicated

She would have been a wonderful mother, a loving wife, a gifted teacher or talented hairdresser. She had incredible talent and she was loved.

I knew that you had every right to remove her from her earthly home. I guess I still I'm not able to accept her absence.

I will not just accept this as sovereign I'm asking you to help me live without her.

CHAPTER 14

The days came and went; the cards stopped coming; the calls all but ceased and we were left with a gaping hole in our hearts and in our home. When Joe would go off to work, I knew he was hurting so deeply, but knew he had to earn a living. (Unfortunately, life does go on and bills have to be paid). The kids would go off to school and I stayed alone. There were times that, like a tsunami, the grief would overwhelm me. It would suddenly come from nowhere. I felt as though I would drown in my sorrow. I knew from past experiences that there was only one place I could turn to find comfort in my grief. I couldn't turn to my husband; he was experiencing the same grief and sorrow I was. Our family too was in the midst of their own pain, and I didn't feel I could burden them. That one place or person I was talking about was the Holy Spirit. I knew He was called the Comforter and, boy, did I need comforting. During these times, when I felt that I would drown in my sorrow and grief, I would sit weeping, sometimes wailing in the family room and I'd cry out to the Holy Spirit to come and comfort me. I would, spiritually speaking, climb on my Abba Father's (another name for the Lord) lap and let Him Hold me in His strong compassionate arms of love till the pain subsided. Yes, He is so very real to me because when no one else could comfort me or soothe my aching heart, He did, through the power and presence of His Holy Spirit.

Other times He used other Christians, who had no idea what I was going through at the time, yet being led by the Holy Spirit, they would be used to minister to me in extraordinary ways. On one occasion, I was weeping before the Lord in our den, which at the time had been my favorite room in the house. It was nicely decorated with white wicker furniture, and it was my special place to read and spend time with the Lord. On this particular day, I was weeping before the Lord. As I wept, I questioned the Lord, "Lord did I do right by my daughter; was I a good mother to her. Lord, I need to know. Lord is she happy?"

As I wept, asking the Lord these questions, our doorbell rang. Our daughter Jeanette, who happened to be home from school, opened the door. I could hear her in the distance speaking with a friend from church, Robin Christian. She asked my daughter to give me a package. Jeanette invited her in, but she declined and left. Jeanette came to the den and gave me the package Robin had left. I opened it and the package contained a cassette (yes, a cassette) and a newspaper clipping with a poem. I began to read the poem and to my amazement one of the questions I had just been asking the Lord was answered in the poem.

I had been asking the Lord "Lord, was I a good parent;

did I do right by Enid?" The poem was entitled TO ALL PARENTS. In it, the writer, who is unknown, is speaking as if God Himself were speaking. I personalized it. "He tells me that He had lent Enid to us for a season. To love her while she was with us and to mourn her when she was gone." He goes on in the poem to tell me that, "she would live six or seven or possibly twenty-two or three years" (our daughter was twenty-two years old when she went home to be with the Lord). The poem goes on to ask if we "would be willing to take care of her till He calls her home." That she "would fill our hearts with great joy (and she did) even though her stay would be brief." Memories of her "would comfort us during our grief." It said that He "couldn't promise that she could stay but that there were lessons that were taught here on earth He wanted His child to learn." My heart leaped for joy when I read the following: He had "looked through the entire world over, searching teachers who were tried and true and from the many people that crowded this earth, He had selected me." As I read this poem, two of my questions were forever settled in my heart. Yes, I had been a good, godly mom, though not perfect, but good enough to have been chosen to be Enid's mom. I recommend you find a copy of this poem and read it. It will bless you, as it did me.

The other question I had was, "Lord, is my baby happy?" The cassette that Robin had given me answered that question. The name of the song on the recording was called: "If You Could See Me Now" originally recorded by a group called Truth. As I heard the words of this song, I was bathed in God's presence and my heart filled with joy. I recommend this song to anyone who has lost a loved one in Christ and is grieving their loss.

The Lord, in His infinite wisdom, knew I needed both the poem and the song. He used a willing vessel to bring the answers right to my door. The Lord once again proved His love and compassion in my hour of greatest need. I will be eternally grateful to Robin for her obedience to the Lord. Grieving takes time, but in order to heal we must be willing to let the Lord walk us through the process.

On one occasion, I was in my daughter's room, sitting on the floor, once again, like a tsunami, waves of sorrow hit my heart. I felt as though I would once again drown in my grief. I had found my daughter's memory box which I had made for her. It was a hat box that I had decorated with peach satin fabric and embellished with beige lace and pearls. I had made it for her to put special memories in. When I opened the box, I had no idea that I would find the first Teddy bear she had gotten when she was born. It had been given to her by her uncle Nelson, who adored her. I didn't know she had it. It was teal green and when you shook it made a jingling sound. It was so badly worn that the fur was just about gone. When you shook it, you could hardly hear it jingle, showing that it had been greatly loved. As I took the little teddy bear in my arms and held it held tightly to my chest, I began to wail. The wailing was so loud that my son Jaysen, who was upstairs in his room, heard me. He came running down the stairs to find his inconsolable mom swaying back and forth weeping uncontrollably. Jaysen took me in his arms and held me. I slowly composed myself, not wanting him to fall apart too. I assured him that I was fine. He waited a while and then went back to his room.

As I sat on the floor, I had a conversation with the Lord (yes you can talk to the Lord, He is always there available to listen to you). This was not a prayer; it was an actual conversation. It went something like this: "Lord it isn't fair, You gifted me with so many talents: I am able to design beautiful floral arrangements; decorate wedding venues. You have allowed me to decorate weddings for family and friends. Yet I was never able to do it for Enid. Lord, I never even got to see her in a wedding gown." As I bemoaned my loss, the Lord gave me a vision. The Lord showed me Enid. She was wearing a beautiful white gown. The gown was made of beautiful satin with a lace overlay, form fitted at the waist. The bodice of the dress was also form fitted and had an off the shoulder neckline. It had a very long train which was attached to the back of the dress. It was magnificent. It was exactly what Enid would have chosen; simple but very elegant. She had a full head of hair which was pinned up on the sides, the way she loved to wear it at times, flowing in long cascades down her back. In her arms she was holding six long stem red roses. She was the most radiant, beautiful bride I had ever seen. Her gaze was fixed straight towards heaven. The gates, made of giant pearls that glistened almost blinding me, opened and she entered in. As the doors of heaven closed behind Enid, the Lord spoke very clearly to my heart: "you've seen your daughter as a bride... My bride." I threw myself face down on the floor and as I wept, I thanked the Lord for His continued faithfulness.

Several weeks had passed and Enid's youth pastor, Pastor Dave Fisher, who had relocated to Boston, came by to visit. He came into the house and began to share his heart with me. He shared how when he heard of Enid's illness, he had made every effort to come to see her but was unable to because at the time he didn't have a vehicle. However, he went on to say, one night he had a dream that caused him to delay his trip. In the dream he had seen Enid. She was standing in our kitchen. She looked completely whole and well. He also noticed that the Lord Jesus was standing behind her and had His arms wrapped around her. He felt a supernatural peace and he believed Enid had been healed. Then he got news that Enid had passed away. He was devastated that he had not gotten to see her one last time. He was so sure that the dream was showing him that she was whole and well, so he felt he could delay his trip. I reassured him that she was totally healed. The dream was showing him that she was in the presence of the Lord. whole and well; completely healed.

Our daughter loved our home. She loved everything about it. I believe her home in heaven is exactly what she loved about our home. She was at home with her Savior safely tucked in His arms of love.

Pastor Dave asked if he would be allowed to go into our daughter's room and just sit quietly there. He entered her room, and I knew he was grieving quietly; I knew he needed that time alone. Shortly after he left, he called me to thank me for comforting him. He remarked that he wanted to comfort me, but that God had used me to comfort him. I gave the Lord the glory for using me in that way. If we are willing, even in the midst of our pain, God can use us to bring comfort to others. Scripture is fulfilled when it says you can comfort those with the same comfort that you yourself have been comforted with. The key is to be a willing and available vessel. What better way to glorify Him and at the same time give the devil a fit? I was determined to give the devil a fit at every turn, naturally, with the Lord's help.

As I mentioned previously, my mother had a hard time handling her granddaughter's death. She loved her dearly and missed her every day. She was one of those who would rarely talk about Enid; I believe it was just too painful. However, one day she came to me and sat down and began to share a dream she had had. You see my mom had always longed to see her grandchildren openly worshiping the Lord. She went on to say that the Lord had given her a dream. In the dream she saw Enid in Heaven. She saw her a little lower than the angels. She had her hands raised up high and she was openly worshiping the Lord. The dream so blessed my mom that she felt a need to share it with me. It was one of the few times my mom spoke openly about Enid after her passing. And the act of sharing her dream served not just to bring healing to her heart, but to bless me tremendously as well, knowing that

God was ministering to my mom's broken heart.

However, one thing constantly nagged at me, which I kept to myself. Lord, I thought, What happened to John 11:4', "this sickness is not unto death but for the glory of God, that the Son of God might be glorified thereby..." (KJV) Our Enid is gone! Lord where is the glory? The one thing that kept me going was the fact that I was not going to allow my grief to paralyze me or the ministry the Lord had entrusted to me. I wanted to get as many young people saved as possible. I wanted to plunder the devil's camp and rescue young people from his grip. So, I threw myself wholeheartedly into ministering to the youth. I knew this was one way of honoring my daughter Enid's memory. The youth loved her and were hurting. I wanted to reassure them that heaven was real and that the God she had put her trust in, had not let her down; she was safely home with Him.

As a mother, sister, friend, and wife, the one thing that was probably the most painful for me to get over, was the fact that after our daughter's passing there was no mention made of her. There were times when I wanted to reminisce about Enid, and I could find no one to speak with. Whenever I mentioned her name to my mom, she would raise her hand to stop me, and the conversation would go no further. Others in the family rarely, if ever, mentioned her name. It was if she had never been born. That was at least how I felt at the time.

As a result of feeling somewhat isolated, the Lord taught me some valuable lessons. First, the Lord taught me to trust in Him totally. He taught me through His Word, through prayer and the power and presence of the Holy Spirit, that He was there 100% of the time. That He truly is "a friend that sticks closer than a brother." Secondly, He taught me be sensitive to the needs of others, especially if they have lost a loved one. If they want talk about their loved one, I was to listen even if I don't have anything to share. Just listening, is possibly all they need. I know that was something I needed desperately but had no outlet. The Lord helped me to understand that for some, it might have been too hard to share openly. That it was possible they were afraid that it would hurt, rather than help me. Having no one to turn to, I chose to speak to the One who always hears and, as I said before, is closer than a brother or any other family member. He loved me through the hard times, the ugly times, and guess what...... He still does!

CHAPTER 15

The first holidays without our daughter weren't easy. Thanksgiving was a blur. I went through the motions. Thanksgiving was always held in our home. This year, for obvious reasons, it was being held at my sisters-in-law's house; just next door. This year there would be no cooking in our home, which was always filled with the smell of desserts baking and the clatter of dishes. Our kitchen this year sat silent as a reminder that things would never be the same again. Thanksgiving came and having nothing to do but show up for dinner, Joe and I drove to what was then K-Mart in Mantua, N.J, just to get out of the house. We wandered from isle to isle not looking for anything in particular, when I remembered that I needed to purchase some 8 x 10 picture frames. Enid's boss's wife Carol had surprised Joe and I with a framed 18 x 24 portrait of Enid, (which appears on the front cover of this book), as well as several 8 x 10 copies. Carol thought we might like to give them to our family. So, our quest became looking for some nice frames for the pictures. We did find the frames, purchased them, and headed home just in time for

Thanksgiving dinner.

Dinner was somewhat different. I know we all had Enid on our minds, but we made the most of our time together. After dinner everyone was gathered together, and I managed to slip away and drove down to my daughter's gravesite. I was intent on just throwing myself on her grave, just to feel Enid close to me once more. As I drove with tears streaming down my eyes, I couldn't understand why the sky was blue, the birds were chirping, life was going on as if nothing had happened. *Doesn't anyone understand that my baby is gone?* I thought.

I got to the cemetery, a small but beautiful place overlooking a lake in Swedesboro, N.J., called Lake Park Cemetery. I got out of my car, still determined to lay down on my daughter's grave. But just then, my gaze was drawn to towards my left. There I saw a family standing, weeping before someone's gravesite. I was shaken to the core and realized for the first time, that I wasn't the only who had lost someone they loved. I came to my senses and stood by my daughters grave quietly weeping and mourning my loss, but thanking God for using another family, who too was mourning, to show me that life really didn't revolve around me. That there were others grieving as well, but that I had to choose to allow His Spirit to comfort me. I got back into my car and returned to my sister-in-law's home, no one being the wiser.

Our first Christmas without Enid could have proven to be filled with great sorrow had it not been for the wonderful youth that I had the privilege of serving. They, along with their families, paid for us to go away for Christmas to Willow Valley Resort and Conference center in Lancaster, PA. It was a great help to get away with our other two beautiful children who had suffered a great loss as well, losing their older sister, and were also mourning in their own way. It was a time of bonding and healing for all of us.

We were able to get through the first holidays without Enid and I continued to minister to the youth. I saw the Lord grow and mature the youth in a mighty way. We saw many of the young people baptized in the Holy Spirit and others recommit their lives to the Lord. I was also privileged to take many of our young people on mission trips with great success. Yet, I still wondered at times why God had given me the Word found in John 11:4, "this sickness is not unto death but for the glory of God, that the Son of God might be glorified thereby..." (KJV), concerning our daughter, and then she went home to be with Him. As an act of faith and obedience I chose to believe that one day He would reveal it to me. I continued to be obedient to the call on my life to touch young people for His glory. Being a faithful Father, He did not disappoint me. One day, in His perfect timing, I was riding with my son Jaysen in the car. Suddenly, I felt a prompting to share with him what I had been feeling for some time about the word the Lord gave me concerning his sister and her home going. I shared how I still had a hard time understanding why the Lord would give this scripture and then take our daughter home. All along, I was standing on this word, believing

He was going to heal her. "Tell me, where is there glory in a twenty-two-year-old girl, with her entire life in front of her, dying?"

Without hesitation, my son began to share what he felt the scripture meant. It was as if the Lord had filled his mouth with His wisdom and as he spoke, the Lord reminded me of the vision I had had several years ago when I was praying alone in church. The vision of the knight which was dressed in black holding a black javelin in his hand. How I was told to rebuke the knight and as I did, the knight backed out slowly, never turning around. I remembered that before he left, he entered the last row on the left hand of the sanctuary where the youth sat. I remembered that was where Enid sat with her friends. As Jaysen spoke he said mom, "Enid was not the intended target, mom, it was you! The devil thought that if he could kill your first born you would curse God and stop serving Him. The chain reaction would have been devastating. None of us would be serving the Lord today, not dad, not I, not Jeanette nor all the young people you have touched for the Lord. God was telling you that the disease that took Enid's life here on earth would not result in your spiritual death, but you would rise up and continue to serve the Lord, thereby He and He alone would be glorified." (These aren't Jaysen's exact words, but this is what I understood him to say as he spoke.) Needless to say, the question about John 11:4, "this sickness is not unto death but for the glory of God, that the Son of God might be glorified thereby..." (KJV), was forever settled in my mind. How awesome that the Lord allowed my son to be the one to reveal to me the answer to the question that so often raced through my mind at times and, if truth be told, tormenting me.

Our son loved his sister, Enid, very much and he wanted to honor her memory. During his time of mourning, he penned a poem which I'd like to share with you. Hopefully, it will be a blessing and encourage young and old alike. It demonstrates that when, yielded to Him, the Lord can use one's grief to bless others.

By Jaysen

```
SHE HAD A BEAUTY BEYOND COMPARE
HER FACE COULD SET A FIRE
THE KINDNESS SHE GAVE WAS HARDLY MATCHED
HER VOICE WAS FROM A CHOIR

THE LIFE SHE LIVED WAS SHORT BUT SWEET
WAS LIKE A ROSE IN THE SUN
THAT GROWS AND BLOOMS FOR A SHORT TIME
THEN ITS TIME IS DONE

HER NAME WAS ENID, MY SISTER, MY FRIEND
ONE DAY SHE WAS STRICKEN WITH DISEASE
THE FUTURE SEEMED CERTAIN, SET AND SAD
YET HER EXISTENCE WILL NEVER CEASE

SHE WENT TO BE WITH HER LORD IN HEAVEN
AND THOUGH I AM FEELING GREAT PAIN
I HAVE AN ASSURANCE IN THAT
I'LL SEE ENID ONCE AGAIN
```

CHAPTER 16

Faithfully, the Lord continued to meet me when my heart ached, and questions would sometimes suddenly overwhelm me. He knew exactly what I needed to hear. One particular Sunday, I was in the front of the sanctuary just sitting in the Lord's presence. I was a little saddened that Sunday when I felt a tap on my shoulder. I was Ron Baus; he owned a car dealership in downtown Swedesboro. He had been recovering from a very severe heart attack that almost claimed his life. I found it strange that we would be in church so soon after having quadruple bypass surgery. Ron sat down next to me and asked if he could share something with me; naturally, I said yes. Ron went on to explain why he had left his sick bed to come and see me. He told me that when he had his heart attack, while in the hospital emergency room and the doctors were working on him, the Lord gave him a message for me. The Lord told him to tell me that Enid was whole and very happy in Heaven with her heavenly Father. As He shared, I knew it was the Lord reminding once again what He had shared many months prior in the song by

Truth, "If You Could See Me Now." He knew I needed the encouragement at that very moment and had used Ron Baus to minister to the sadness I was feeling just then, proving to me yet once again that He was always there with me.

As I continued to trust the Lord, He continued to faithfully unravel other questions I had. I remember one time during prayer, I asked something of the Lord not knowing if it was even possible. I asked the Lord, if somehow, I could let my beautiful daughter know that we were fine and that I was still in ministry serving Him with great joy. I just threw that question out there not knowing whether that would ever come to pass. Years came and went and one day I got a call from my closest friend, Phyllis. Phyllis had a childhood friend, Gail, whom she adored. Gail had been diagnosed with terminal brain cancer. Phyllis wanted us to go and pray with her. I agreed to go, however, I told Phyllis that we needed to be sensitive to her friend's needs. I agreed to pray for Gail, but first, if given the opportunity, I wanted to ask her how she would want us to pray.

We arrived at Gail's home. Her husband Johnny directed us up to their guest bedroom. Gail was in bed. She was an absolutely stunning woman. She looked so radiant, if you didn't know it, you would never guess she was terminal. We visited for a while and then I asked if there was a specific way she wanted me to pray for her. Without hesitation, she asked that we pray that her departure from here to eternity would be as smooth as possible and that the Lord would comfort her husband and her children. We then knew she wanted to go home to be with her Lord and Savior. Gail then turned to my friend Phyllis, whose husband Jim had passed away a year prior to my daughter and asked her the following question, "Phyllis, when I get to heaven, is there anything you want me to say to Jim when I see him?" I can honestly say I don't recall if Phyllis responded, because no sooner than Gail had asked Phyllis that question, that she turned to me and said, "Ruth, I know you have a daughter in Heaven. Is there anything you'd like for me to say to her?" I held back my emotions and my tears. With a knot in my throat, I responded: "Yes, please tell her that we are all well and are all serving the Lord and one day we will be together again."

We visited with Gail for a little while longer. Before we left, we prayed for her as she had directed. As we prayed, we felt the presence of the Lord fill her bedroom. It was glorious. We knew that Gail was ready to go home with her Savior. When I got in the car, I began to cry, and Phyllis asked me what was wrong. I shared with her the question I had asked the Lord seven years earlier, not knowing if it was even possible. Yet here I am having this simple request answered. I was simply awe struck by His capacity to love me so much, that He gave me the opportunity to come to visit with Gail, not so much for her benefit but for mine.

As often happens there was a change of guards in our Church. Pastor Petrucci was called to minister in a church in Delaware. After months of searching, a new pastor was installed. Pastor Donnachie, the new pastor, having heard about our daughter Enid, decided to go to the cemetery and stand in a couple moments of silence at her grave. Try as he might, he couldn't find her grave. As he was getting ready to give up the search, he heard the "still small voice" of the Lord say to him, "Why are you looking for the living among the dead?" With that he turned around and left the cemetery. That so impacted him that he told me of his experience. That encounter with the Lord by Pastor Donnachie so encouraged my heart. Here, many years later, our daughter was still impacting lives and the Lord is being glorified thereby.

There have been other instances where my Savior has spoken to me over and over again concerning my beautiful daughter. Today I can say without a doubt, as I quote John 11:4 "this sickness is not unto death but for the glory of God, that the Son of God might be glorified thereby..." (KJV), our daughter Enid's disease has not been unto death. For every day that Joe and I live and share our faith in the One, the only True God, He is glorified. The Lord has proven Himself faithful to His promises in our lives.

I've had the privilege over the years to share our story of triumph in the midst of great loss. My God was my source of strength and continues to be so. My journey is not yet over but I have a full assurance, that as I continue to trust in Him totally, He and He alone will continue to fill me with His peace and assurance. That, just as David said when his son died in 2 Samuel 12:23, "But now that he is dead, why should I go on fasting? Can I bring him back again? I will go to him, but he will not return to me." I, too, have said and continue to say, while my daughter Enid was alive, I fasted and I prayed, but she is now in heaven with the Lord. Enid can never return to me here on earth and I certainly wouldn't want her to. This is the assurance I have that one day I will go to her. And together, after I have cast my crown at my Father's feet and worshiped Him, Enid and I will walk hands-in-hand on the streets of gold. Till then, it is my privilege to be His vessel to be used as He sees fit, so that the Scripture He gave me so long ago, John 11:4: "this sickness is not unto death but for the glory of God, that the Son of God might be glorified thereby..." (KJV), would continue to resonate in my life and the life of those who knew our daughter and now know my story; this is Not Unto Death!

EPILOGUE

I'd like to take a moment of your time to share a couple of lessons I learned as I went through this journey. Hopefully they will be of some help if ever you or someone you love goes through a similar journey.

Don't Make Assumptions

What do I mean when I say, don't make assumptions? Let me first give you the definition of assumption: Merriam-Webster's dictionary defines assumption as follows: an assuming that something is true; a mistaken assumption.

When the Lord spoke John 11:4 "this sickness is not unto death, but for the glory of God, that the Son of God might be glorified thereby." (KJV) to me, I took it and ran with it. It was the anchor which kept me going through the whole ordeal. However, I had assumed that Enid would be healed: I was wrong. My error in making this assumption caused me many years of questioning why the Lord had given me that Word, yet Enid had not been healed. Years later, when the Lord knew that I was ready to fully receive what He meant by it, He revealed it to me, using my son Jaysen to explain the meaning of this powerful word, as I described previously in the book.

So, my advice is: don't make assumptions. When you get a Word, you believe is from the Lord, seek godly counsel. Be willing to listen and apply the advice received, always making sure it lines up with the Word of God.

Test the voice you may be hearing

As I wrote in the book, during our daughter Enid's 22nd birthday celebration I heard an audible voice say, and I quote; "This will be the last birthday you will celebrate for Enid." I immediately took a spiritual posture and rebuked what I thought was the voice of the devil. In retrospect, I believe it was the Lord speaking to me. He was trying to prepare me for what was to come. However, I was not willing to even entertain that thought for a moment because that would mean that I had misheard the Lord when I received the word from, John 11:4, "this sickness is not unto death, but for the glory of God, that the Son of God might be glorified thereby." (KJV) I never shared this with anyone. Looking back, I probably didn't want anyone to dissuade me from what I believed. I learned not to let pride keep me from asking Godly counsel. I probably could've avoided many mistakes I made along the way.

Always submit to the Lord

My prayers were not answered as I desired but I, along with my husband Joe, chose to submit to the Lord and accepted His answer. With our submission came the necessary peace which we both needed, as a couple and individually, to continue to not only serve Him but love Him and openly proclaim His goodness and His keeping grace. As a result, yes, I have seen and continue to see John 11:4 "this sickness is not unto death, but for the glory of God, that the Son of God might be glorified thereby" .... (KJV), fulfilled in our lives.

Allow yourself to grieve

Joe and I mourned our daughter together and separately. We allowed the Lord to take us on that journey. It was painful but very necessary, as I noted in the book. However, mourning given entirely to the Lord brings with it healing. It gives, and gave, us the ability to thrust ourselves into the arms of the only one who understood; and He gave us beauty for ashes. We, Joe and I, have an assurance that eternity holds with it a family reunion with our precious daughter.

I recommend, that if you've lost someone you love, be it a husband, a child or another loved one, give yourself the time to mourn. But make sure you also give yourself the gift of healing. If you stay stuck in your mourning it will ultimately rob you of the joy that the Lord intended for you to experience. God's love is greater than your pain and is able to heal your broken heart. The key is you must let Him do so. Find trusted people who you can talk with, cry with, and pray with. As you do, you will come out on the other side of mourning and experience the joy you need to live a victorious life. Who knows if one day you might be given the opportunity and privilege of comforting someone with the same comfort you were comforted with?

Make precious memories

Life is like a vapor, as the book of James so aptly puts it in, James 4:14, "What is life? It is even a vapor that appears for a little while and then vanishes away."

Remember to take time to be with loved ones; enjoy their company. Those memories, as aptly stated in the poem ("To All Parents") I shared in this book, will be solace during your time of grieving. Those memories will bring a smile to your face when that special someone comes to your mind. So, take time to make special memories with those you love.

Final Words

As parents, we will all be faced at some point in our lives that ill-fated moment we most dread; the talk. You know, your child is getting to that age where you feel it appropriate to talk to them about what is often referred to as "the birds and the bees." Somehow, we never really had that conversation with Enid; not on a personal, one-on-one basis. As a youth pastor, I was very open with our young people concerning sexual purity. Enid was an integral part of the youth group, so she did know the importance of sexual purity.

I know some Christian parents prepare in advance to speak to their child about sexual purity. Many times, the young person is taken out on a date with the dad. After having the talk, dad might offer his child, male or female, a promise ring to be taken off on their wedding day; a symbol to be given to their husband or wife that they are coming into their married life sexually pure.

I found myself, instead of talking to our daughter about her sexuality, talking to her about a topic no parent is really prepared to talk about. I was sitting next to her in Cooper Hospital in Camden, having a conversation I never, in my wildest dreams, thought I would have. We were discussing the subject of death and dying. Enid was still fighting a valiant fight, but I saw her strength diminishing day-to-day. I needed to know how she felt about death and dying. It may sound morbid, but it was by the Lord's prompting that this conversation took place.

Shortly after she had been transferred to Cooper Hospital to be prepared for her transplant, we were alone in her room. Enid was lying very still in her bed. I wanted to assure myself that she was okay, so I gently touched her shoulder. She shrugged and turned towards me. I mustered the courage and asked her how she felt about death and dying. Enid didn't hesitate. She quickly answered. "No mom, I'm not afraid of dying, I'm afraid of what it will take to get me to the other side."

I thought that was so profound. We will all face death someday. I imagine, if truth be told, no more legitimate answer has ever been given. What will we, individually, have to go through before we enter glory?

Thankfully, Enid knew her Savior would walk her

through the valley called death. I reassured her Jesus would be there every step of the way. I believe that was why her favorite passage of scripture was Psalm 23. Somehow, she knew she would be walking through the Valley of The Shadow of Death at a young age. I'm so grateful she had an assurance she was saved and redeemed. So many aren't. I pray that as you read this dialogue between my daughter and I, you would make Christ your Savior, so that at the end of this journey called life, you too will be safely escorted home to the other side. There may be pain in the journey, but eternity is waiting, and it is glorious.

If you'd like to invite Christ into your life and want Him to be your Lord and Savior, simply pray the following:

Lord God, I recognize I need a Savior. I know that I can never be good enough to gain a place in heaven. So, I invite you into my life. Forgive me of my sins and become my Savior. I pray this in Jesus's name, amen.

So simple, yet so profound. If you've prayed that simple prayer, you have just reserved your place in eternity. Now, go find a good church where you can be ministered to and grow in your faith.

CPSIA information can be obtained
at www.ICGtesting.com
Printed in the USA
BVHW092243270922
648002BV00002B/11